INTERIOR
LANDSCAPING

INTERIOR LANDSCAPING

Tok Furuta

ILLUSTRATIONS
Debra Sievers
Vernon Artman

RESTON PUBLISHING COMPANY, INC.
A Prentice-Hall Company
RESTON, VIRGINIA

Library of Congress Cataloging in Publication Data

Furuta, Tokuji.
  Interior landscaping.

  Bibliography: p.
  Includes index.
  1. House plants in interior decoration. 2. Indoor
gardening. I. Sievers, Debra. II. Artman, Vernon.
III. Title.
SB419.F98 1983   747'.98   82-15043
ISBN 0-8359-3120-X

Editorial/production supervision and interior design
by Barbara J. Gardetto

© 1983 by
Reston Publishing Company, Inc.
A Prentice-Hall Company
Reston, Virginia 22090

10 9 8 7 6 5 4 3

Printed in the United States of America

DEDICATED TO BETTIE L. FURUTA

Table of Contents

Chapter Three
THE GROWTH OF PLANTS 39

Chapter Four
THE INTERIOR LANDSCAPE ENVIRONMENT 65

Chapter Five
HORTICULTURAL CONSIDERATIONS BEFORE INSTALLATION 83

Chapter Six
PRINCIPLES OF INTERIOR LANDSCAPE MAINTENANCE 97

Chapter Seven
PLANTS FOR THE INTERIOR LANDSCAPE 129

Acknowledgments

A book such as this simply does not happen. This book is the culmination of years of study and thought. During this period, I gathered ideas and thoughts from many places and people. I synthesized the ideas and thoughts into the present set of recommendations and explanations.

Among the many people in the commercial and university fields and in the U.S. Department of Agriculture who have been influential, I would like to acknowledge Alex Laurie, former professor of Floriculture, Ohio State University, as having a great influence. Many contemporaries, such as Marc Cathey and Charles Conover, are sources of important ideas and principles. Perhaps the most influential were the many nameless faces that asked questions, raised points of issue, and presented ideas for discussion. They made the development of sound reasoning necessary.

Preface

Have you seen, felt, or heard a good interior planting lately? Have you stopped to look at people as they sit among plants indoors? Have you thought of a wonderful and restful location as you contemplated a single plant in your home or office? This is what it is all about, this book on interior landscaping or interior plantscaping.

Plants have been used indoors ever since people moved indoors. Plants filled an emotional and spiritual need then. They do so today. From the tropics to the Arctic and Antarctic circles, plants of many types are used indoors. The plant may be a tropical specimen or it may be the top of a carrot or pineapple. Whatever the origin or type, plants are necessary in our environment.

What, then, is new in recent years about the use of plants indoors? An awakening understanding of the various roles that a plant or a planting play in human terms is the most important new discovery. At one time, plants were considered to play only an esthetic role. But with the movement toward open offices, that is, the office without permanent walls and with only furniture and plants to define space and its use, plants took on

another meaning. Plants helped to define spaces of various uses. Plants controlled the flow of traffic, screened views, reduced glare from windows.
What is new?

- Plants have become a status symbol in many offices. "I am important enough for plants to be placed in my office by the company."

- We more fully understand the emotional needs that are satisfied by plants in the interior environment.

- An awakening interest in developing planting and maintenance systems that are easy to care for. Techniques to take away some of the mystique of the "green thumb" have been perfected. Planting systems have been developed that tell one when to add water and how much to add.

- A better understanding of plants and how we can care for them indoors.

- The specialist who designs interior plantings, installs them, and arranges for their care.

- The search for a name to describe this profession.

- The need for information and assistance. And that is the purpose of this book, to provide information about interior landscaping.

The types of information needed by successful interior landscapers are many. A certain amount of information about plants, how they function, grow, and survive, how they react to environment, and how they are affected by adversities, is needed to ensure proper care. This book provides the information needed to understand plants and their growth. However, it is not the intent of this book to present detailed physiological information; such information is better found in specialized books devoted only to this aspect.

This book concentrates on the horticultural aspects of design, installation, and care of an interior planting. Tips and facts are given to ease the burden of caring for such plantings.

This book also provides some information about plant species and varieties. (The names of plants follow the reference Hortus III.) It departs from the usual in that legend and other interesting facts about plants are given. This information can be used to increase appreciation about plants among the clients of the interior landscaping business.

Finally, this book talks about design and plants from a human aspect. This latter point is little understood. It is hoped that more and more studies will be conducted in this area of understanding.

This book provides the basis for designing beautiful interior plantings that meet human needs, and for proper installation and maintenance. With the information in this book, it will be possible to do an acceptable job. On the other hand, each chapter could be expanded into a larger and more detailed volume. With this book the student may begin the study of this subject; from this beginning, he and she may greatly increase his or her knowledge about plants, and about people.

Tok Furuta

INTERIOR
LANDSCAPING

CHAPTER ONE
Introduction to Interior Landscaping

Hardly a shopping mall, bank, or office building is without plants. The use of plants extends to the individual office and home; people have always had plants around them indoors. Recent plantings have differed from those of the past in that design and thought, professional advice, and the hiring of professionals have been a part of the design, installation, and maintenance of attractive interior landscapes.

Attractive interior landscape plantings are not a luxury or an impossibility. The application of a few fundamental principles, the giving of regular care, close observation of plant response, and the use of a large measure of common sense are needed. Attempting to become too precise or too technical usually results in more problems than solutions.

Attractive interior landscapes involve many considerations that begin before the planting is made. Ideally, interior planting should be considered when the building is being designed. Many problems associated with the

Attractive interior landscapes are dependent upon (1) properly designed situations, (2) proper installation of the plantings, (3) an understanding of what people other than those charged with care of the planting can or should do, and (4) informed personnel that have complete charge of caring for the plantings.

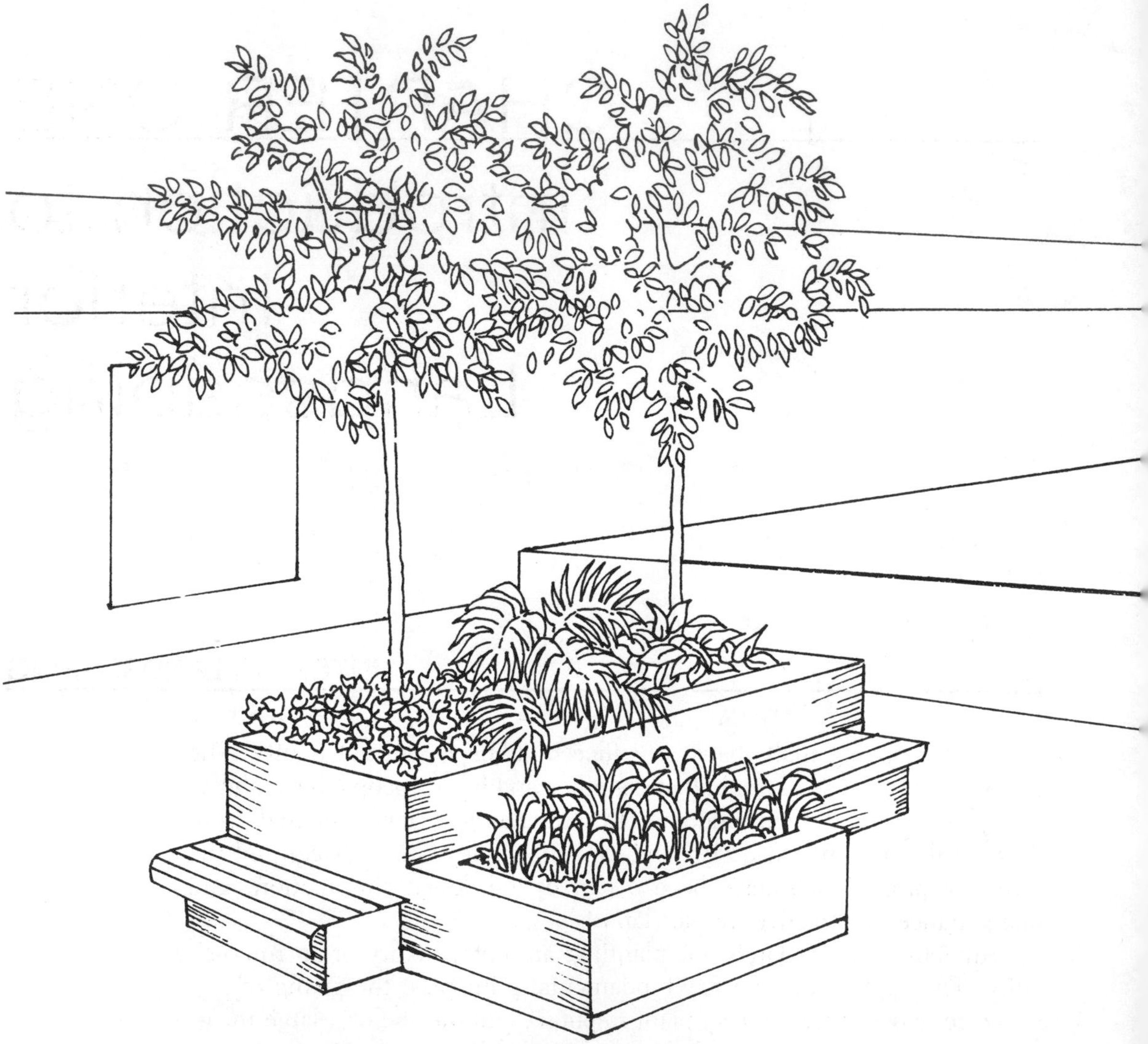

FIGURE 1–1
**Planting in shopping mall creates restful sitting
area, divides space, and enhances the vista.
Properly placed plantings eliminate the long,
tunnel effect of the main corridor of the mall.**

FIGURE 1–2
Planter in corner to add elegance and a restful
feeling to the office. Plant color and form
harmonize with office decor. Container does not
detract from plant. Light intensity must be
adequate for healthy plants. If natural lighting is
not sufficient, electric lights must be turned on
the plants.

FIGURE 1–3
Plantings appear differently depending on the viewpoint. Different emotions can be evoked depending on the viewpoint.

maintenance of plantings are due to the architects and designers of the building omitting vital details.

PLANTS ARE NOT FOREVER

We should approach interior landscaping as another appropriate application of plants in our environment. As such, we must accept the fact that plants have a beginning in life, grow older, mature, and finally die. The life cycle may be for a few days, a few months, or for many years (see Figure 1–4).

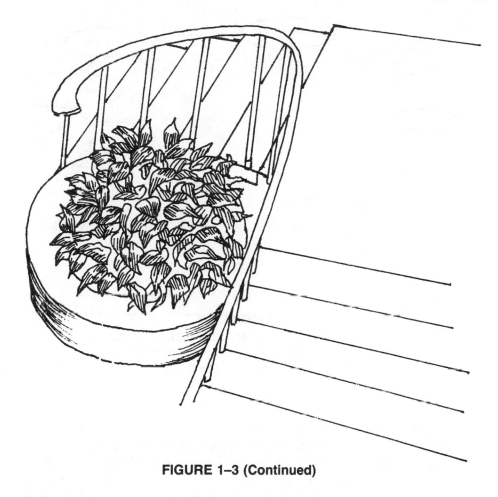

FIGURE 1–3 (Continued)

Some of the plants we value for interior landscapes are used because of attractive or distinctive juvenile growth. Examples include *Epipremnum aureum (Pothos aureus, Scindapsus aureus)*, a common interior plant, and *Dizygotheca elegantissima*, the spider aralia.

With some plants, both the juvenile and mature forms are used. However, the two forms have very different characteristics and would present different design characteristics. In fact, often in the trade the two forms of the same plant may be called by different names. For example, a slow-growing plant commonly called Swiss cheese, *Monstera deliciosa*, has large leaves that are cut and have oblong holes in the mature stage. In the juvenile form the leaves are not as large, have fewer divisions, and no holes in the leaves. The plant grows rapidly as a vine in the juvenile stage. The juvenile form of *Monstera deliciosa* (Figure 1–5) is often sold as *"Phil odendron pertusum."*

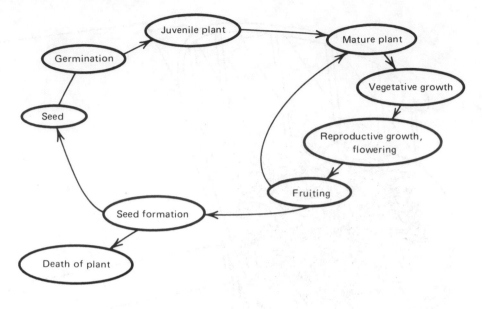

FIGURE 1–4
The life cycle of plants, germination to death,
may be a few days or hundreds of years
depending on the plant.

Not only must we expect to replace plants as they mature and pass effectiveness, but we must expect to replace plants that are used for some special effect. Flowering plants are used in interior landscapes because of flower color. Chrysanthemums in flower are effective for about three weeks; then they should be removed. Other plants are used for seasonal effect and should be removed when the season is over—poinsettia for Christmas and the Easter lily for Easter, for example.

Replacing plants as a regular part of maintaining the interior landscape gives the added benefit of an attractive and effective planting. It will reduce the maintenance problems and should lead to better public relations and employee morale.

HANDLING COMPLEXITIES

As we begin our study into the use of plants in peoples' environment within buildings, we should recognize that plants have been used in such locations for many years. Someone will have tried almost every suggestion of something new we can give. New plants, new methods of irrigation, new methods of controlling pests, all these and more have probably been

(a) Juvenile growth of *Monstera deliciosa*

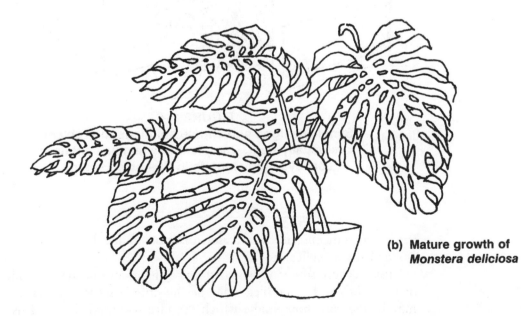

(b) Mature growth of *Monstera deliciosa*

FIGURE 1–5
Plants differ in shape, size, color and growth
between juvenile and mature stages.

7

FIGURE 1–6
Simple designs and simple solutions to problems
are usually best. One plant in a simple container
conveys many moods in this office setting.

tried; and someone, for one reason or another, has labeled the idea un-workable or inapplicable.

Just because someone has tried and failed does not make an idea bad or unworkable. The problem may be the criteria set for evaluation, or it may be the conditions under which the idea was tried. Each of us might look at the same set of data and draw widely varying conclusions. Or we may come back to the same set from time to time and have different opinions each time.

Planning, installing, and maintaining interior landscapes are complex activities, but at the same time they can be relatively simple. We must learn to handle the complexities at the appropriate time with as much simplicity as possible.

OUR ENVIRONMENTAL SYSTEM

The purpose of the interior landscape is to create a more pleasing environment. At the same time, plantings may be placed in a manner to help control some of our actions. The way people relate to the environment we

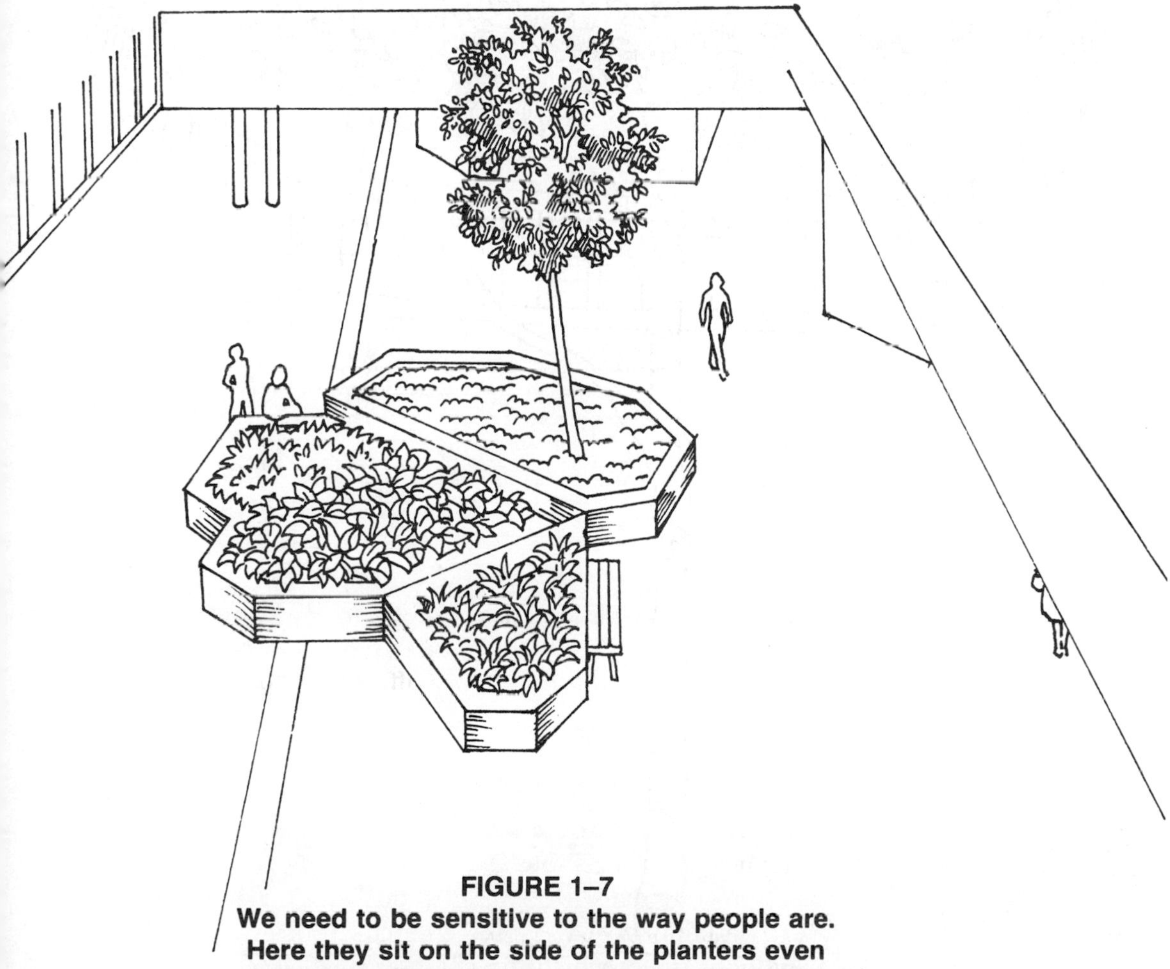

FIGURE 1–7
We need to be sensitive to the way people are. Here they sit on the side of the planters even though seating benches exist a few feet away. Plantings along the edge of the planter can and have been damaged. Proper design and maintenance will eliminate plantings made unattractive by people acting naturally.

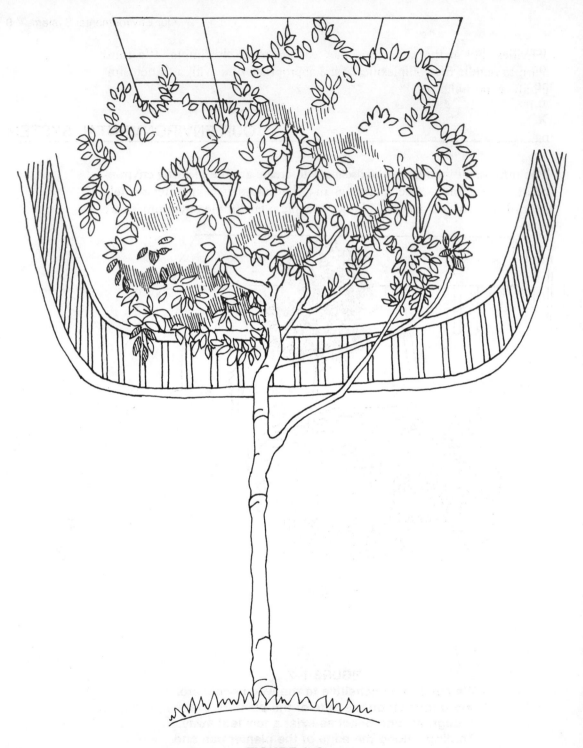

FIGURE 1–8
A better and more pleasing interior environment
because plants were tastefully and simply used.

create and use the elements we place in the environment are of prime importance to us. Signs and barriers will not change people's ways of using the elements. For example, we have many times observed people sitting on pots and the sides of planters both in and out of doors in planted areas. Design and plantings should take this into consideration and provide seating areas. We must be sensitive to others' use of the environment.

Many scientists consider the understanding of people's environments of utmost importance in understanding the people. Being aware of their environment and the significance of the environment brings us to a better understanding of the people involved. We can determine more precisely their life-style, philosophy, and much more.

Most people will respect good facilities and take care of their environment. Challenge them with a fortress and a group of people will be moved to assault the fortress. Give them a pleasing environment to protect, and they will protect it.

Whether the interior landscape does in fact create a better and more pleasing environment is the ultimate test of our effectiveness as designers and horticulturists.

CHAPTER TWO
People and Interior Landscaping

Plants serve as symbols and have many functional uses. In addition to the symbolic uses of keeping people in tune and in contact with nature, the functional uses of plants are esthetic, architectural, engineering, sensual, and climatic (see Table 2–1). Outdoor landscape plantings, the design of which has been studied for many years, have long incorporated many of these uses and symbolic meanings. True, not all the possible uses or symbols have been delineated or verbalized, but somehow the end result has been fairly satisfactory. At least we have been able to measure their impact in that we can observe whether the landscaped developments have in fact been used and the nature of the use.

Plants indoors in interior landscapes serve as the same symbols and perform the same functions, with the possible exception of controlling the climate of the interior. However, the interior landscape designer does not have the space to bring in grandiose plantings. Thus, the use of plants indoors must often suggest or have one plant do the job of a more dense

TABLE 2–1
Purposes Served by Plants Indoors

USE	FUNCTION
Emotional and symbolic	• Maintain a person's contact with nature
	• Mentally and emotionally carry a person to an unspoiled environment
Sensual	• Mood delineators
	• Sounds, odors, touch feelings stimulated, enhanced, gratified
Architectural	• Control of privacy
	• Screening of unpleasant views
	• Progressive realization of views
	• Articulate space
Engineering	• Control of traffic
	• Reduction of glare
	• Acoustical control
Esthetic	• Background
	• Sculpture
	• Line calligraphy
	• Softening architecture
	• Frame views

planting outdoors. It is possible by careful placement to achieve the desired results. For example, one or a few plants can divert the flow of traffic and control it in a manner that will speed flow or bring the traffic into a place of interest.

SYMBOLIC AND EMOTIONAL USES OF PLANTS

There is no unanimity as to how a plant specifically fills symbolic and emotional needs, but the presence of plants and the need to give them care have been of enormous emotional value to people. Some claim that people have a primal instinct for the need of plants in the environment, that there is a hereditary need. Others may dispute this without discounting the fact that plants serve or fulfill a tremendous emotional need in people. Hardly a day goes by that we individually do not associate with plants in our environment, plants that are there not to provide food, shelter, or clothing, but just plants in the environment. This is true even for those who do not consciously associate with plants.

Even above the Arctic Circle, where the sun does not rise all winter long and people must live under the glare of electric lights, plants are grown for the emotional benefits provided by their presence. The same is true of scientific expeditions to Antarctica. Plants are taken along or seeds are sprouted.

Plants and people interact in a positive way so that people receive positive emotional benefits. In this connection, it may not be totally important to determine whether there is a latent programmed need or whether there are positive personalities in plants. More important is that people interact with plants in their own and positive way; this alone makes plants worthwhile.

It is perhaps in the philosophy that underlies and is the basis for the culture and appreciation of plants grown as bonsai that the symbolic use of plants is most highly developed and recognized. For those who understand bonsai, viewing a single bonsai scene mentally and emotionally transports the individual to a seaside, mountain, or some other natural and emotionally satisfying location. Here the individual is able to commune with nature and to gain inner strength from such close association.

INDIVIDUAL COMMITMENT TO PLANTS

Individuals have varying degrees of commitment to having plants in the interior environment. At one extreme are those who claim to dislike plants and would just as soon not have them around. On the other extreme are those who are very emotionally involved with plants and think of them as living things with personalities. Major groups between the extremes include those who have low emotional involvement but think of plants as having personalities, and those who have a high emotional involvement, but think of plants not as living items with personality but as decorative items. (See Table 2–2.)

Each major group of people (people and plant relationship) may present different problems concerning designing for plants and the program of maintenance. What is the motive of the person ordering the plants and how will he or she react to actions of the installers and maintainers?

TABLE 2–2
Some Ways People Relate to Plants in Their Environment

GROUPING	INVOLVEMENT WITH PLANTS	BEHAVIOR CHARACTERISTICS
1	Emotionally involved with plants, believing that plants have personalities and are not just decoration.	Loves to take care of plants. Usually has many plants of many sizes and states of health. Would rather propagate plants and nurture sick plants back to health than acquire large specimens. However, will purchase many plants, often on impulse with little regard to price.
2	Emotionally involved with plants, but uses and keeps them for their decorative effect, to keep the person in the swing or the forefront. Plants used for their snobbish appeal. Plants do not have personality.	Invests in many plants, acquiring large specimens and very conscious of quality. Demands high quality. Often swayed by the unique, but will seldom buy on impulse; very much price conscious.
3	Not emotionally involved with plants, but considers plants as living individuals with personalities, that they are not decoration only.	Has a few plants, usually acquired as gifts. Wants to keep plants healthy, but seldom buys plants. When purchases, usually buys small sizes.
4	Not involved emotionally with plants, has them only as decoration. To them plants do not have personalities.	Purchases a few large plants, often at a low price, but plants must have high quality. Considers care for plants definitely a chore.

SENSUAL USES OF PLANTS

Plants help to create the mood for an interior. This would be through the type of plants, which by touch, sight, or smell, will trigger varying moods in the inhabitants, depending upon their personalities and past associations with plants. Cactus and succulents can create the mood of being in a hot, arid location. Palms, orchids, bromeliads, and tropical vines may create the peaceful mood of a tropical beach under a full moon. They might also recall the tropical jungle with its insects, animals, and dangers.

Most sensual feelings must depend upon sight and touch. Sound may be used occasionally by adding the sound of water. Sounds of wind and birds would be difficult to add; tape recordings are too monotonous. Smell may occasionally be used; plants with different scents can be brought in on a rotating basis.

In the end, it is the mood created in the mind of each individual that counts. The same mood may not—probably will not—be created in all. What is simply a pleasant scene to one may be, because of feel and sight of the plants, an extremely stimulating scene to another. Leaves velvety to the touch or moist red smooth leaves stimulate sensuous feelings. Leaves shaped in the outline of a heart may trigger other thoughts.

ARCHITECTURAL USES OF PLANTS

Among the principles of using plants in landscape development are their use to screen, to partially conceal and to articulate or divide space into separate areas. In the design and construction of buildings without permanent, or even temporary, floor-to-ceiling walls, designers have used plants, furniture, and screens to divide interiors into distinct "offices" and other work areas.

Other architectural uses (see Figure 2–1) would include (1) softening harsh lines, (2) screening undesirable views indoors or out, (3) partially screening desirable views to entice and enhance the enjoyment of seeing the view, and (4) privacy, by screening the area from undesirable viewing.

ENGINEERING USES

Engineers are usually concerned with traffic, sound, glare, air conditioning, and filtration of air (see Figure 2–2). Plants indoors can be used to control or partially overcome some problems caused by engineering concerns. Plants may partially or completely screen glare from lights or windows. Plants may be placed in a manner to control and direct traffic. Plants may aid in reducing sound; however, much more information is needed before definitive answers can be given.

ESTHETIC USES

The esthetic qualities of plants have long been recognized by interior designers and others. In fact, to some people, this is the only reason

(a) Divide space

(b) Privacy

FIGURE 2–1
Architectural uses of plants.

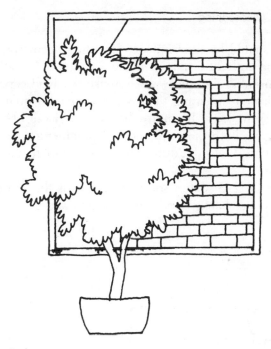

(c) Screening unpleasant views

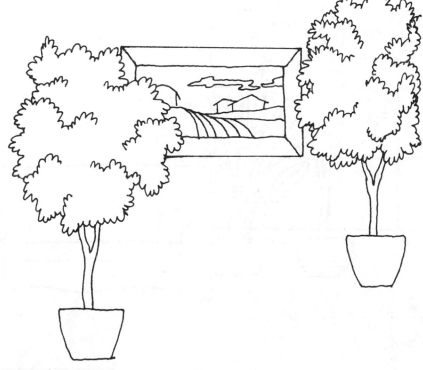

(d) Partial screening

FIGURE 2–1 (Continued)

plants should be used indoors—for their decorative and esthetic qualities.

The authentic uses of plants in interior situations cannot ignore the elements of design necessary to make any landscape, piece of furniture, or artwork more pleasing. The same principles hold true for interior landscapes; simplicity, harmony, balance, and the like cannot be ignored. In this regard, both the plant and the container are elements to use in interior decoration. Color, texture, and shape must fit the design scheme for the interior.

Figure 2–3 shows some examples of the esthetic uses of plants—as sculpture, as background, and to soften and control.

(a) **Control glare**

FIGURE 2–2
Engineering uses of plants.

(b) Control of traffic

FIGURE 2–2 (Continued)

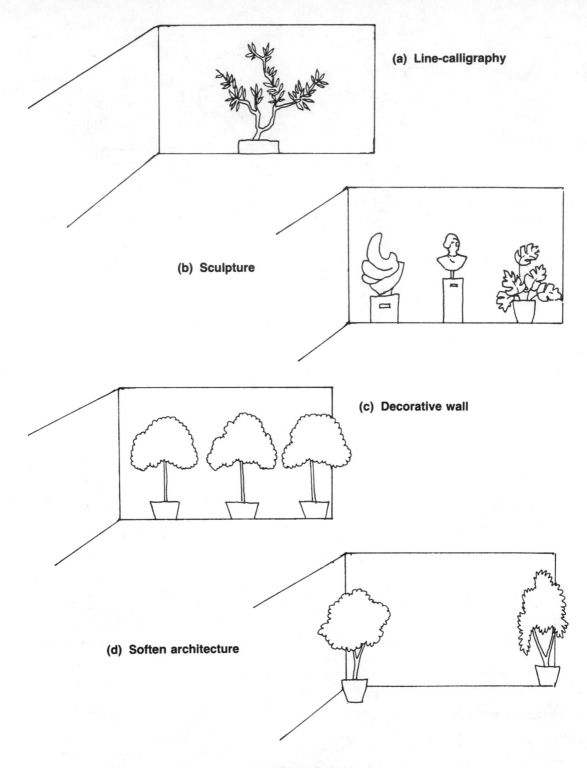

(a) Line-calligraphy

(b) Sculpture

(c) Decorative wall

(d) Soften architecture

FIGURE 2–3
Esthetic uses of plants.

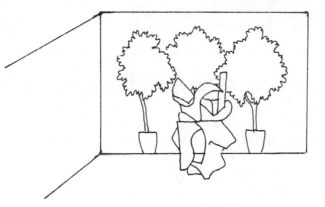

(e) Pattern, silhouette

(f) Control view—gradual revealing of vista

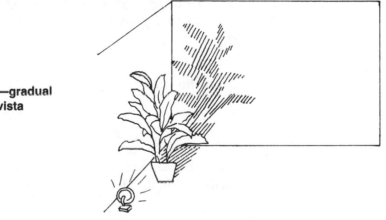

(g) Background

FIGURE 2–3 (Continued)

TIPS ON DESIGN

Designing the interior landscape should create moods and organize the space. When organizing the space, the impact of the design and subsequent spaces must be considered. Landscapes will not be completed upon installation. Rather they are constantly growing, changing, and presenting different pictures and evoking different moods each day. The ability of the individual to design interior landscapes improves with experience. Each subsequent design will be better and more pleasing.

The design must be based upon sound principles. The different aspects of design may be studied separately, but in the end, the total effect, the total feel of the design is important. This feel comes from a skillful blending of the various aspects of design. Table 2–3 is a summary of design considerations.

The Feel of the Land

Many designers—from landscape architects to interior designers—consider most important the preliminary analysis to get the feel of the land before beginning to solve the problems of effective design for the interior space. One active landscape architect goes so far as to spend time alone at the location—to sit on the mountain top and feel all the parts through all

TABLE 2–3
The Various Aspects of Design

Design is:

- a problem-solving activity. For example, control the view, control the flow of traffic, and provide decoration for an ugly corner.

- a creative activity. Individuals express their creativity through the designs they develop.

Planting designs:

- exist for people. People are alike yet different, unable to change yet constantly changing, lowly yet with heads in the stars. People are unique, wonderful, unpredictable. Without people, there would be no need for design.

- exist in both space and time. Plants constantly change in appearance—hour to hour, noon to night—because the quality of light affects our perception. Plants grow, mature, and eventually die.

TABLE 2–4
To Design Effectively, Get the Feel of the Land

FACTORS TO CONSIDER
Offices:
- Personalities of the people in the office
- Image they want to project
- Their involvement with plants

Public Places, Such as Shopping Centers, Restaurants, or Banks:
- Predominant type of clientele (modern and savvy, middle American, or young and far out)
- Image projected by owners and managers

his senses. Once this study is completed, the placement of the various parts of the interior landscape becomes simpler; the parts fit easily together.

To obtain the feel of the land, factors such as people and the use of the area must be considered. Not only the people who work in the area, but also the clientele, must be considered. Designs appropriate for middle America are not appropriate for the leaders in art or business. For example, exotic designs are not appealing to middle America.

Table 2–4 lists factors to consider when trying to obtain the feel of the land.

Types of Designs

Generally, two types of design are recognized: (1) formal or symmetrical and (2) informal or natural or asymmetrical. Both types of design are useful. Informal designs are often more difficult to execute. Attention must be paid to growth and change over time. Figure 2–4 shows some elements of both design types.

Design Affects Humans by Causing Responses

All people are affected by the design of a given space. Specific responses are influenced by background, education, religion, and other personal attributes. However, in general, certain predictable results are ob-

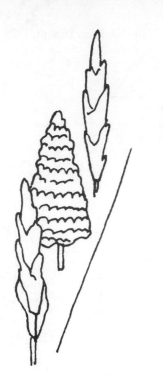

- Straight lines
- Square or rectangular forms
- A formal plant shape
- Same elements on both sides of the axis
- Balance due to same element on each side of axis
- Philosophy: people dominate nature

(a) Formal

- Curved lines
- Soft, round forms
- Natural plant shapes
- Different elements on each side of axis
- Balance due to sum of attraction on each side of axis
- Philosophy: people are a part of nature

(b) Informal or Naturalistic

FIGURE 2–4
Types of design.

tained from such considerations as form, types of lines, and colors. Designers of interior spaces should be aware of these reactions and not create undesirable reactions by the improper use of design elements. (See Table 2–5 below.)

TABLE 2–5
How Specific Human Responses Are Achieved

HUMAN RESPONSE	DESIGN PRINCIPLES	HOW DESIGN ELEMENTS ARE USED
Relaxation	Familiarity and simplicity; to "think round thoughts."	Flowing lines; curvilinear focus; stable structures; quiet colors (white, gray, blue, green).
Contemplation	Allow subject to withdraw. Design is mild and unpretentious. Scale is not important.	Forms not insinuating nor are contrasts sharp. Soft, diffused light; misty, tranquil, and recessive colors.
Awe	Overwhelming scale.	Soaring forms contrast with the horizontal colors of chaste white or cool and detached (blue-green, green, violet).
Sensuous love	Privacy; inward orientation; intimate scale.	Intimate space with soft, round forms, female forms, exotic elements. Colors of soft rosy pink to golden.
Gaiety	Free space with rhythm and movement.	Smooth, flowing spaces and patterns. Warm, bright glowing colors and lights.
Dynamic action	Bold forms.	Structural cadence heavy; use of angular planes. Colors are strong, primitive (crimson, scarlet, yellow-orange).
Tension	Unstable forms and illogical complexities.	Split compositions; clash of colors; wide range of values of color; no relief from intense colors.
Fright	Sensed confinement; facing the unfamiliar.	No point of orientation; dim, dark, eerie; abnormal monochromatic colors (cold blue, cold greens).

TABLE 2–6
Lines in Design Can Evoke Human Response

EMOTIONAL RESPONSE	TYPE OF LINE	
Passive	Soft, straight line	
Feminine	Flowing, soft curves	
Active	Sharp angles	
Dynamic	Strong, sharp angles	
Bold	Strong curves	
Stable	Right angles	
Unstable	Oblique angles	
Uncertain	Wandering lines	
Fleeing	Moving away from point	
Brutal	Strong, illogical angles	

- Two-dimensional, static experience
- Changing location of viewer does not change perception of object
- Apprehend object consciously from without
- Example: viewing espalier plant against wall experience

(a) Pictorial

- Three-dimensional experience
- Stereoscopic experience
- Changing location changes perception of object
- Apprehend object consciously from without
- Example: viewing free-standing plant in a container

(b) Plastic

- Three-dimensional experience
- Kinetic (dynamic or moving) experience
- Apprehend object subconsciously from within object
- Example: inside an enclosure of plants

(c) Spatial

FIGURE 2–5
Types of human involvement with interior landscapes.

FIGURE 2–6
Patterns created by planters and plants when
observed from above can evoke intellectual and
emotional responses.

Viewing an object or design from without invokes certain emotions. The emotions may be from viewing a two-dimensional design, such as a silhouette or a mirror image of a plant. Different characteristics occur when a plant is seen in three dimensions. Here, the viewpoint is important.

Involvement in the interior landscape means that human beings are inside the space where plants are used. Most of the design of interior landscapes will include involvement from within the design, while at the same time viewing one or more elements of the design pictorially or plastically.

Some of the responses and effects achieved through design are given in Tables 2–5 and 2–6. Figures 2–5 and 2–6 demonstrate types of human involvement.

Elements of Organized Space

The entire interior space is a three-dimensional space with floor or ground plane, side or walls, and a ceiling or sky. Plants will be used in at least two of these parts of the space, the walls or side plane and the ceiling or overhead plane. Indoors, plants are seldom used as a floor covering; interior landscapes differ from outdoor space in this regard. Plants may be used as a covering on the ground level, but these will be areas where people will not enter—areas for visual appearance only. Figures 2–7 and 2–8 present some elements of spatial design.

Plant Characteristics

When all is said and done, the interior landscaper must analyze the different design aspects of the plants that are available. These aspects are listed in Table 2–8.

The characteristics of a plant may change over a period of time as it grows in the interior landscape. For example, many variegated leaves or colorful leaves will gradually turn all green in interior situations. The reason is that color develops under relatively high light conditions, and interior conditions generally lack sufficient light for intensive color to develop. Similarly, flowering may not occur under interior conditions.

When plant characteristics cannot be maintained over a period of time in the interior location, the choices available are to substitute a more adapted plant with similar characteristics or to modify the environment so that the plant can maintain the desired characteristic. Either choice will often require imagination and innovative thinking. In light of the need to conserve energy, the choice often is to use more adapted plants.

TABLE 2–7
Some Principles of Composition

SIMPLICITY	• *Keep it simple.* Use as few plants and objects as possible. The more you use, the more complex the relationships:
	
	  a. Use two elements ( ), have one relationship
	
	  b. Use three elements ( ), have three relationships
	
	  c. Use four elements ( ), have six relationships

UNITY	• *It hangs together* or *"I like it"* • Proper proportion and relationships of elements • Ugliness when sensed lack of unity exists • Ugliness when incongruous elements are present
SCALE	• Relate size of plants and objects to humans • Too large, it overpowers; people feel insignificant • Too small, it is ineffectual; in small space, people feel cramped, irritated

PROPORTION	• Relative size of part to the whole
	• Some formulas:
	  a. Two horizontal to one vertical
	  b. The golden triangle (side measures are 3–4–5)
	
	  c. Do not divide space into equal sizes

BALANCE	• Sensed balance around an axis
	  a. Formal balance: same elements on each side
	
	  b. Natural balance: sum of attractions (color, number, size, etc.) on each side balanced

TABLE 2–7 (Continued)

SEQUENCE   •   Succession of objects and feelings for interest

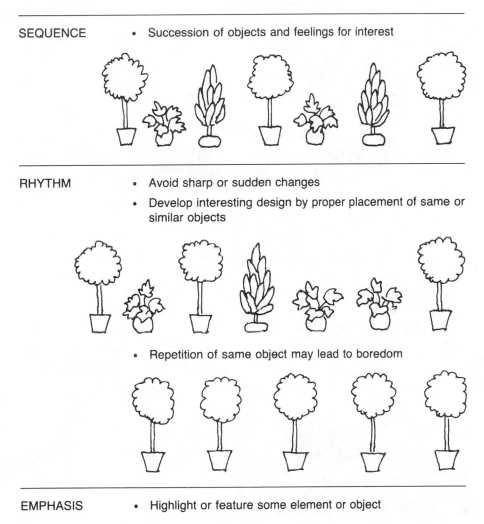

RHYTHM   •   Avoid sharp or sudden changes

                 •   Develop interesting design by proper placement of same or similar objects

                 •   Repetition of same object may lead to boredom

EMPHASIS   •   Highlight or feature some element or object

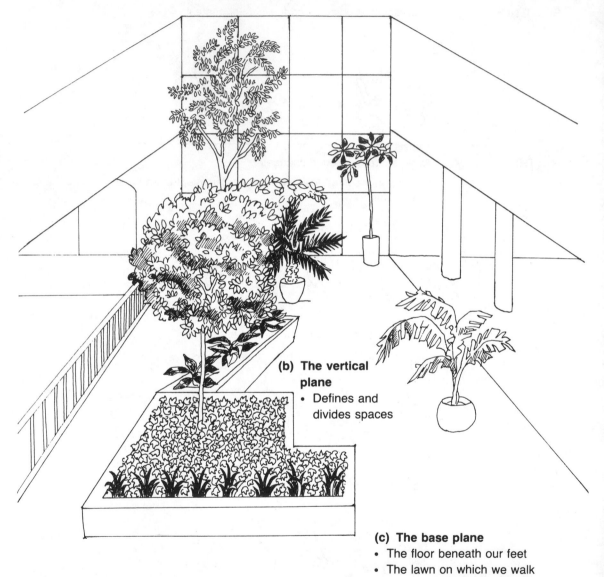

(a) The overhead plane
- gives height control
- suggests control of light
- suggests control of environment
- gives airy feeling of sky

(b) The vertical plane
- Defines and divides spaces

(c) The base plane
- The floor beneath our feet
- The lawn on which we walk
- The base on which patterns of plants and planters placed

**FIGURE 2–7
The elements of organized space from use of plants indoors.**

Category	Appearance	Examples
(a) Mass Oval, spreading		• *Rosa hybrids* and miniature
Rounded		• *Pittosporum tobira* • *Cyclamen persicum*
(b) Line Linear, upright		• *Sansevieria trifasciata*
Linear, spreading		• *Philodendron x wend-imbe* • *Asplenium nidus*
Linear, curved		• *Spathiphyllum clevelandii* • *Dracaena fragrans* • *Howea forsterana*
Cascading		• *Sedum morganianum* • *Nephrolepis exaltata* bostoniensis
(c) Exotic Weeping		• *Ficus benjamina*
Picturesque		• *Coccoloba uvifera* • *Chamaedorea erumpens* • *Monstera deliciosa*

FIGURE 2–8
Forms or shapes of plants for interior landscapes.

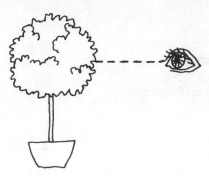

(a) Pix
- Eye level, 5 feet when person is standing, 3 when sitting
- Place feature of greatest interest at this level

(b) The pull of the harbor
- The growing and gradual revealing of the scene pulls one into the harbor

(c) Outward thrust that repulses

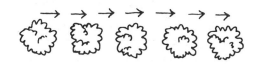

(d) Straight lines
- Lack interest—lead to monotony

(e) Power of suggestion
- The mind multiplies the possibilities, expands the scope and richness

FIGURE 2–9
Some elements of spatial design.

(g) Gradual revealing
- To see all at once is not the purpose

(f) The vista

Coarse texture makes an object appear nearer

Fine texture makes an object appear farther away

Converging lines usually add distance

Diverging lines usually shorten distance

(h) Apparent or visual distance
- Space may be visually changed by use of the elements

FIGURE 2–9 (Continued)

TABLE 2–8
Characteristics of Plants Used in Interior Plantings

COLOR	• Keep variation to minimum, especially in small spaces
	• Consider color of all parts—leaves, stems, flowers, fruits, and so on
	• Color can change due to interior environment
	• Consider seasonal changes
SHAPE OR FORM	• Usually will use three-dimensional aspect (plastic); often can create a two-dimensional picture (pictorial) by using shadows, silhouettes, and reflections
	• The shape of the plant naturally or as controlled by the grower
TEXTURE	• Does the plant appear fine or coarse?
FRAGRANCE	• Avoid unpleasant odors
	• Avoid conflicting fragrances
SIZE	• At the effective stage
	• Changes over period of time
LONGEVITY	• Might depend on skill of the maintenance people

CHAPTER THREE
The Growth
of Plants

A plant in any environment perceives and reacts to the amount or intensity of each of many separate factors, such as light, temperature, and air movement. All the separate factors are integrated into the plant growth that we see.

Each factor exerts separate influences on plant growth. Various factors together exert influences that are interrelated; response to one factor is influenced by the presence and intensity of another. For example, plants in low light conditions are injured by fertilizer dosages that would be suboptimal at high light conditions.

From a practical viewpoint, for plants indoors, water, temperature, and light are the primary considerations. One of three approaches to a site is possible: (1) temperature or light may be adjusted for the plants, (2) the plants must adapt to what exists, or (3) a combination of the first two approaches may be possible. The solution used depends on considerations in addition to the plant and plant growth. But to come to the best solution requires a knowledge of plants and plant growth.

DIVERSE NATURE OF PLANTS

Individuals from many parts of the plant kingdom are used for interior landscaping. They come from different habitats and are complex biological organisms. Plant taxonomists arrange all plants from the simplest one-cell organism to the most complex, highly specialized individual into 15 different groups called phyla (singular, phylum). These groups were developed on the concept of a logical evolutionary development of the reproductive structures. The first and lowest class consists of single-cell plants; to reproduce the cell simply divides. Examples are bacteria and algae. Specialized cells, tissues, and organs do not exist.

Virtually all the plants used for interior landscaping are in the highest plant phylum. See Table 3–1. All classes and subclasses are represented.

For the purposes of interior landscaping, it is not necessary to be a plant taxonomist. It is important, however, to know the differences in plants depending on their classification.

TABLE 3–1
Typical Examples of Different Botanical Classes of Plants Used for Interior Landscapes

	TYPICAL REPRESENTATIVE INDOORS
ferns	• Boston fern, *Nephrolepis exaltata* Bostoniensis • Staghorn fern, *Platycerium bifurcatum*
cone-bearing seed plants	• Norfolk Island pine, *Araucaria heterophylla* (*A. excelsa*) • Sago palm, *Cycas revoluta*
flower-bearing seed plants	
Monocots	• Common scrub pine, *Pandanus utilis* • Paradise palm, *Howea forsterana* • Philodendron • Bromeliad • Wandering Jew
Dicots	• Weeping fig, *Ficus benjamina* • Grape ivy, *Cissus rhombifolia*

While in general every plant has similar anatomical structures and responds to the environment in similar ways, specific differences exist. These differences may profoundly affect one's satisfaction with the plant or may influence a plant's reaction to the care given by maintenance people. For example, some palms such as the Paradise palm *(Howea forsterana)* do not have lateral buds and will not branch; thus cutting off the main shoot kills the plant. On the other hand, the Lady palm *(Rhapis excelsa)* branches and forms a clump. The branching of this palm differs from the branching of a fig tree, however. These examples illustrate the need to identify the growth characteristics of each species of plant. They also illustrate the dangers of simplification and generalization about plants.

WHAT IS PLANT GROWTH?

For our purposes, plant growth may be described as an increase in the size of the plant. The increase in size is not reversible. However, it is possible to have larger plants, that is, taller or wider, without increasing the weight.

All plants are composed of many cells. As plants grow, the number of cells increases. This increase is the result of cell division, a process in which cells split to form two where one existed before. Cell division occurs in meristems.

Following division, cells increase in size and eventually become specialized cells for the various functions needed for the survival of the individual. The increase in size of all the cells produces the enlargement, which we term plant growth. Enlargement of cells occurs in areas adjacent to the meristems.

Meristems

Meristem means "capable of dividing." In these regions, cell division occurs. In general, we define three principal meristem areas for plants: apical, intercalary, and lateral. Other meristems exist in specialized individuals.

An apical meristem is that located at the apex or tip of a shoot or root. Each shoot or root is tipped with a meristem. In apical meristems the cell division that occurs results in growth in length.

Intercalary meristems occur in shoots at the nodes or, in the case of grasses, at the base of the leaf. Growth in length results from cell division and elongation in these areas.

As the term implies, lateral meristems are along the side. Specifically, the cambium is the lateral meristem for plants. Increased diameter of shoots and roots is the result of cell division in lateral meristems.

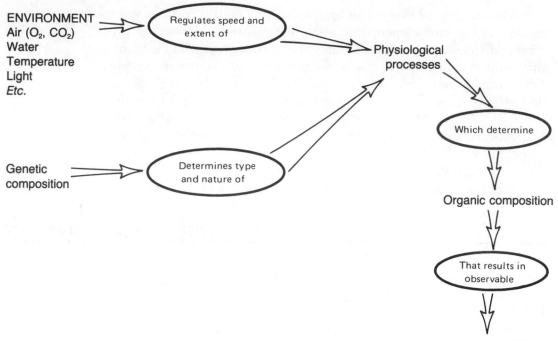

FIGURE 3–1
Interaction of environment and genetic
composition in influencing plant growth.

METHODS FOR CONTROLLING
PLANT GROWTH

Throughout the history of our use of plants for food, fiber, and environment, the control of the type and nature of plant growth has been achieved. We have learned that each plant has a potential for growth determined by inheritance. The genetic control is part of the organism and sets the upper limits. To change these limits requires a change in the genetic makeup, which is achieved by controlled hybridization.

Altering the genetic makeup of a plant is only one of many methods of altering or controlling plant growth. Some methods may have a permanent effect, while others are temporary. An example of a permanent effect is a dwarf plant resulting from grafting a plant onto a dwarfing rootstock. A temporary method can be the dwarfing of plants by pruning. Stop pruning and the plant grows to full size.

TABLE 3–2
Methods to Control Plant Growth

METHOD	RESULT
Hybridization	Alters genetic composition, resulting in a permanent change. May require many generations to achieve results. Examples include dwarf plants and new leaf colors.
Mutation	Induces genetic changes by chemical or other means. Effect permanent. May require many years for results. Changed plant must be propagated asexually. Examples include new flower colors, leaf colors, habit of growth.
Grafting (and budding)	Desired top (scion) placed on rootstock to achieve dwarfing, resistance to root diseases, etc. Effect is permanent. Could be used more for indoor plants.
Chemicals	Chemicals may alter growth such as stem elongation and number of branches. Chemicals must be registered for use on plants in interior locations; very few have been. Effect is temporary because, unless death occurs, plant outgrows effect of chemical. Chemicals usually sprayed on. Some are effective as soil drenches where absorption by root occurs. Not commonly used on interior foliage plants.
Environmental	Altering environment changes plant responses and the resulting growth we see. Various factors can be altered simultaneously to achieve desired growth or to evaluate growth to be satisfactory under poor or stressful conditions. Effect temporary because restoring the altered factors to optimum enables plant to resume normal growth. Environmental manipulation alters rate of growth.
Physical (pruning, wiring, etc.)	Removing portions of the plant or bending shoots to grow in desired direction. Shape and size of plant altered, but rate of growth unchanged. Changes are permanent, although later growth may hide the change. Therefore, continuation of practice is necessary.

Control of plant growth may be achieved by chemical and physical methods. The accompanying Tables 3–2 through 3–4 discuss the principal methods. The desired result, the cost, and when the control measure is to be applied are the determining considerations for selecting the procedure to be used.

TABLE 3–3
Some Ways to Achieve Specific Types
of Plant Growth Control

TO CONTROL:	PROCEDURES TO ACHIEVE
Plant size	• Genetic dwarfs or small plants • Grafting (budding) onto dwarfing rootstock • Chemicals to reduce growth, provided chemical is safe to use and registered for use • Pruning; must be done on a continuous basis for most effectiveness • Reduce nutritional levels and less frequent irrigations
Plant shape	• Pruning to remove undesirable shoots, leaves, etc., must be practiced on a continuing basis • Chemicals to prevent undesirable growth provided chemical is registered for use and is safe to use • Bending, retraining, and otherwise physically altering direction of shoot growth
Retard or reduce leaf fall	• Deciduous plants allowed to develop leaves indoors • Condition plants for interior location by growing in low light and nutrition condition • Maintain low and balanced nutritional levels • Do not allow plants to suffer from lack of water • Chemical to retard abscission, provided chemical is registered for use
Stimulate shoots to grow in specific locations	• Girdle shoot. The girdle may be partially or completely around shoot. Does not work with many plants; shoots will die. • Chemical applied to buds, provided registered for use • If buds lacking, grafting or budding can be done with certain plants
Prevent growth of buds	• Chemical sprayed or painted on desired area
Shorten internode length	• Chemicals known as growth retardants may be used • Higher light intensities (brighter lights), where practical

TABLE 3-4
Guide to Pruning Practices with Plants
in Interior Environments

The objective is to control the size of the plant and its shape. Because plants in interior environments are observed at close range, the art of pruning must be practiced to enhance the beauty of the plant.

OBJECTIVE	PROCEDURE
Maintain the plant size or to allow slow increase in size of plant	Cut or pinch each new shoot as it grows. Up to one-half of the new growth is removed. As new shoot grows, it is pinched. This practice must be done regularly.
Shorten a shoot without a lateral shoot.	Cut the shoot ¼ inch above a node or bud.
Shorten a shoot to a lateral shoot	Cut the shoot close to and above the lateral shoot and make a slant cut.
Remove a lateral shoot	Cut off lateral flush with main shoot.
Thin out the top	Remove lateral shoots, leaving the main shoots intact.
Reduce the size of the plant	Cut back the shoots to a lateral shoot or remove them completely to the main trunk. Keep in mind the shape desired when the shoots have been removed.
Train plant to a particular shape	Prune out unwanted shoots and pinch others to encourage branching.
Encourage branching	Cut back shoots to a bud.
Remove leaves at time plant is transplanted	Thin out lateral shoots and remove leaves only.
Encourage branched roots	Cut roots to desired length.
Overcome pot-bound or circling roots	Cut all roots at surface of root ball. Roots are completely removed.

(continued on following page)

TABLE 3–4 (Continued)

Remove a large lateral limb	Cut the shoot off in stages to prevent ugly tears in the bark of the trunk. Proceed as follows:

1. Make a cut under the limb about 6 inches from the trunk. Cut upward about one-third of the way through limb.

2. Cut tree limb off, making the cut about 4 inches out from the first cut. The result is a stub.

3. Remove stub completely, close to trunk.
   a. Find branch bark ridge.
   b. Cut down and away from trunk.

4. Use knife to clean up rough areas.

5. Coat the wound with shellac. Tree seal may be used if color is not objectionable. *Never use lead-based or oil paints.*

Remove a broken branch	Cut off below the broken area to a node or a lateral shoot.
Remove a shoot torn off the stem	Cut the wound area with a knife to make a clean, oval-shaped wound. Then coat with shellac.

TEMPERATURE AND PLANT GROWTH

We usually consider temperatures of freezing or below to be necessary for plants to be injured by the cold. The degree of cold that a particular plant species can withstand depends on its origin. Most plants used indoors will not withstand many degrees below freezing.

Different parts of the plant will withstand different degrees of freezing temperatures; roots are killed at lower temperatures than are leaves and shoots. In addition, the stage of growth is important; actively growing plants are injured at higher temperatures than dormant plants. See Figure 3–2.

Tropical plants and others are also subject to chilling injury. At cold temperatures above freezing, cells are killed even though ice does not form in the tissue. Chilling injury occurs at temperatures from freezing (32°F or 0°C) to about 45°F (5 to 6°C).

Above the temperatures where chilling injury occurs, plant growth gradually improves until an optimum temperature is found. Each type of growth (flowering, stem elongation, etc.) may have a specific optimum temperature range. Thus, some plants will not flower well if the temperatures are in the fifties and will flower well in the sixties. Stem growth, however, may be good at both ranges, although slower at the lower temperature.

PLANT REACTIONS TO DIFFERENT TEMPERATURES

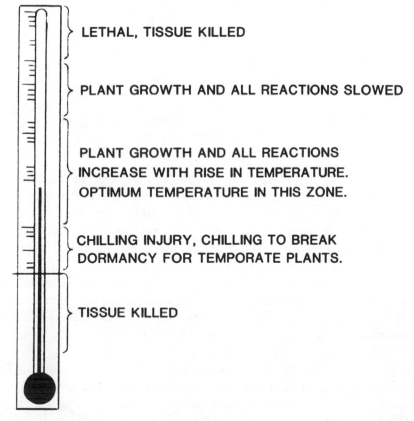

LETHAL, TISSUE KILLED

PLANT GROWTH AND ALL REACTIONS SLOWED

PLANT GROWTH AND ALL REACTIONS INCREASE WITH RISE IN TEMPERATURE. OPTIMUM TEMPERATURE IN THIS ZONE.

CHILLING INJURY, CHILLING TO BREAK DORMANCY FOR TEMPORATE PLANTS.

TISSUE KILLED

FIGURE 3–2

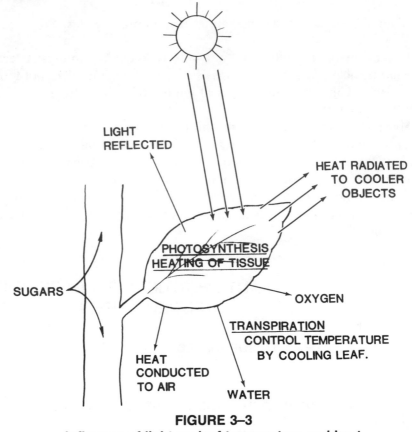

FIGURE 3–3
Influence of light on leaf temperature and heat
exchange from that leaf.

Temperatures in the optimum range and for some degrees on each side influence the rate or speed with which reactions and growth occur. Thus, raising the temperature 10°C (18°F) results in doubling the rate of photosynthesis, provided that all other factors such as light intensity, water, and carbon dioxide supply are not limiting. The rate of respiration will also increase two to two and one-half times.

Above the optimum range, plant growth becomes slower as temperatures continue to increase. Eventually, a lethal temperature is reached.

It is the temperature of the plant tissue (leaves, stems, roots, etc.) that is important. Usually the tissue temperature is the same or very closely the same as the air temperature surrounding the plant. However, many occasions may arise when the tissue temperature is different from the air temperature. Three such situations are when (1) the leaf is exposed to direct sunlight, (2) the leaf or tissue is exposed to an infrared heating source, and (3) the tissue or leaf is directly exposed to a clear, cold sky in the winter, as through the clear window of the room. See Figure 3–3.

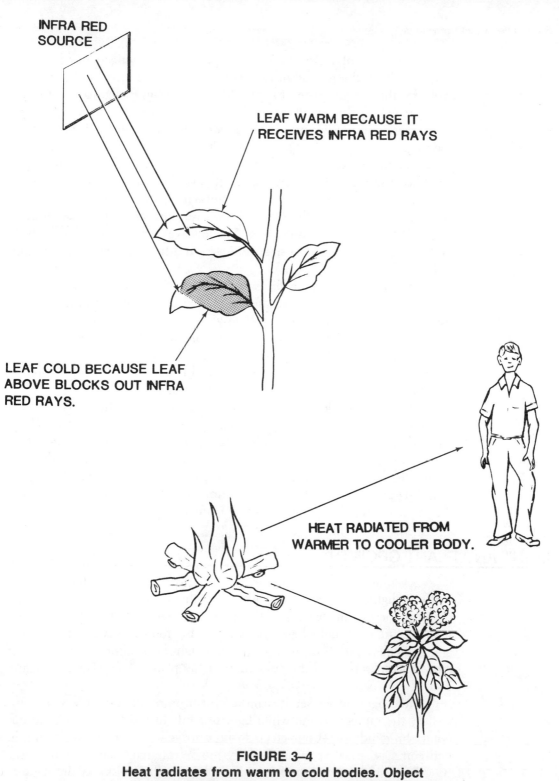

INFRA RED SOURCE

LEAF WARM BECAUSE IT RECEIVES INFRA RED RAYS

LEAF COLD BECAUSE LEAF ABOVE BLOCKS OUT INFRA RED RAYS.

HEAT RADIATED FROM WARMER TO COOLER BODY.

FIGURE 3–4
Heat radiates from warm to cold bodies. Object
must "see" heat source to be warmed.

When sunlight strikes the leaf of a plant, part is reflected and the rest is absorbed. Of the part absorbed, part is used in the process of photosynthesis for the manufacture of sugars. Part of the light is converted to heat energy; some of this energy is used to influence the rate of transpiration, the evaporation of water into vapors that diffuse out of the leaf through the openings known as stomata. If sufficient amounts of water are available, the leaf remains relatively cool at only a few degrees above air temperature, because energy is used to convert water to water vapor. If water is deficient, or with some large-leaved plants, no matter what the water supply, the temperature of the leaf will increase until a lethal temperature is reached. This results in sun scorch. Shade leaves scorch more rapidly than sun leaves, probably due to size, thinness, and thin cell walls. See Figure 3–4.

Infrared heating acts in the same manner. Infrared rays (that is, heat rays) are absorbed by the leaf and converted into heat to warm the leaf. Infrared rays are not effective in photosynthesis. Infrared radiation may not trigger the mechanism that results in the opening of the stomata, the minute pores in the leaf through which water vapor diffuses during the process of transpiration. The heat of the leaf will be reradiated to colder objects and conducted into the air surrounding the leaf.

Warmer objects lose heat to colder objects by conduction if the objects are in contact or by radiation if the objects are separated in space. Thus, on cold, clear nights, leaves can lose heat to the cold sky through radiation loss. Fortunately, the leaf is able to absorb heat from the surrounding air so that the leaf temperature will be only a few degrees colder than the surrounding air. This usually is not a serious problem unless the air is near the temperature where chilling injury occurs.

LIGHT AND PLANT GROWTH

Without light, green plants as we know them will not exist. Light has many influences on plant growth, among which is photosynthesis or the manufacture or carbohydrates that serve as the food supply for the plant— and ultimately for all of the animal life. Light also influences the type of growth we observe and the coloration of the plants. See Figures 3–5 and 3–6.

White light, as we see it, can be broken into different colors. For instance, the rainbow is the white light of sunlight broken into the various colors by raindrops—from green to blue to yellow to red, and colors in between.

Plants respond not to white light but to the colors of light. The

TABLE 3–5
Relative Response of Plants to Different Colors of Light

Name	Wave Length in Nanometers	Plant Process, Relative Response[a]				
					Photomorphogenesis	
		Chlorophyll Synthesis	Photosynthesis	Phototropism	Inductive	Reversal
Violet	350–400	0	0	80	5	0
	400–425	25	50	60	5	0
Blue	425–450	60	100	90	5	0
	450–475	30	50	80	5	0
Green	475–500	5	30	40	5	0
	500–550	10	20	0	5	0
Yellow	550–600	20	15	0	20	0
Orange	600–625	25	20	0	30	0
	625–650	90	30	0	50	5
Red	650–675	60	60	0	100	0
	675–700	0	40	0	30	30
Far red	700–750	0	0	0	0	100
Peak responses at (wave length)		445 and 650	435 and 675	370, 445, and 475	660	710 and 730

Note: Depending on where and how individual plant species and varieties evolved, their response to color may differ markedly from these general responses. Many plants used in interior landscapes evolved in shady conditions; their response to color differs from that given in this table.

[a]Arbitrary units.

amount of energy required for a plant reaction to occur differs with the color of light. Generally, the most active light color, that is, the color producing the greatest response to a small change in light energy, is red. The second most active color is blue. Plants are relatively insensitive to yellow light and quite insensitive to green light. See Table 3–5.

The reaction of individual plant species to different colors of light will depend on where and how the species evolved. The reaction of plants that evolved under dense shady conditions (many tropical plants used for interior landscaping fall in this category) will differ from those that evolved under sunny conditions. Plants evolving under shady conditions will be more reactive to blue, because reds have been filtered out by leaves overhead.

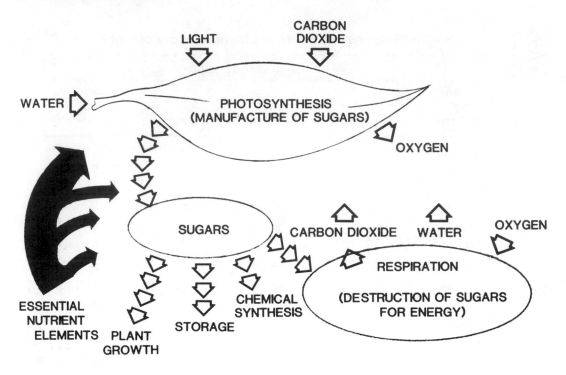

FIGURE 3–5
Manufacture and use of sugars by green plants.
The relative rates of the various processes
depend upon, to a large extent, the amount of
raw materials available and the temperature
surrounding the plant.

Photosynthesis, the manufacture of carbohydrates, requires light in addition to water, carbon dioxide, and the presence of chlorophyll—the green coloration of plants. This process will occur in low light intensities; however, at low light intensities the amount of carbohydrates manufactured by the plant is small. In addition to the amount of light or light intensity, the length of daylight is important in determining the total amount of food manufactured. Plants kept in low light conditions are able to manufacture enough food to sustain life, provided that steps are taken to also limit the use of food.

Food in plants, that is, carbohydrates, is used for four purposes. First, food is used for growth, the building up of the cells of the plant as the plant grows, that is, the number of leaves, the length of the stem, the diameter of the stem, for flowering, and so on. Second, excess food, that

Light Intensity	Plant responses
Excessive	Sun scalding occurs
High	Optimum level of light: • Production of carbohydrates at a high level, respiration normal. A lot of the carbohydrates stored by the plant. • Variegated leaf color intense. • Leaves small, thick. • Leaves close together.
Medium	Suboptimal level of light: • Production of carbohydrates reduced, respiration normal resulting, in less quantities of carbohydrates stored. • Variegated leaf color less Intense. • Green color more intense. • Leaf larger, thinner. • Stem thinner, leaves more widely spaced.
Low	• Light compensation point; production of carbohydrates equals that used in respiration. • Low levels of light; plant survives on stored carbohydrates.
Total Darkness	• Green plants will not survive continued darkness.

FIGURE 3–6
General reactions of plants to changing light intensity. Specific light intensities at which different reactions occur depend upon the species.

Environmental factors plus genetic makeup of the plant influences the rates and kinds of physiological processes that determine observed plant growth.

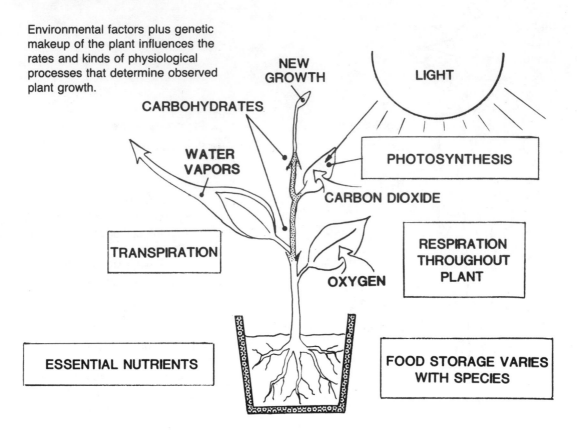

FIGURE 3–7
Where green plants obtain the raw materials needed for growth and survival and where major processes occur in the plant.

food not needed to sustain life and to add to the size of the plant, is stored. Third, food is used to form all the needed organic compounds. Fourth, food is used in the process of respiration to supply the energy needed to sustain the life of the plant.

Whenever the manufacture of food does not equal the demand for food, the plant must use food that is in storage. When the storage is used up, the plant must and does use the compounds found in the more mature tissues and organs to sustain the life and growth of the younger and developing tissue. These new growths become sinks that draw the food away from the more mature tissue, even to the point where the older tissue suffers deficiencies.

Sun leaves, that is, leaves that develop in high light intensities, are thicker than shade leaves. Placed in low light conditions, sun leaves may abscise (fall off the plant) rapidly. Shade leaves may not fall off because they developed in low light intensity conditions.

Light also influences the *direction that the leaves and stems grow*. That plants grow toward the light is a common observation. This is the result of the action of light on the hormonal concentration on the sides of the stem. Hormonal concentration influences the amount of enlargement of the cells. The cells in the stem away from the light become larger, causing the stem to bend toward the light. When the light is equal on all sides of the stem, the hormonal concentration is equal, and the stem grows in a straight line.

SHOOTS WILL GROW TOWARDS LIGHT
ROOTS WILL GROW AWAY FROM LIGHT

FIGURE 3–8
One-directional light and plant growth.

The *duration of light* or day length influences many plant reactions, such as flowering and the amount of vegetative growth, all other factors essential for growth being optimally present. Plants such as chrysanthemums and poinsettias will not flower unless the daylight length is short. Plants such as jacaranda grow much more rapidly when the daylight length is long.

Light intensity not only influences the amount of food manufactured by the plant and the direction of growth of the shoots and roots; it also influences the *thickness of the stem and leaves* and the distance between leaves on a shoot. Growth of shoots under low light conditions will result in thin stems with widely spaced leaves. The stems may not be strong enough to hold the plant erect.

Also, different structures within the leaf are affected. The leaves developing in reduced light intensity conditions, as in a building, will be thin and have thin cell walls. The green matter (chloroplasts) that carries out the process of photosynthesis is arranged in a horizontal manner, as contrasted to a stacked manner when leaves develop under high light intensity. This horizontal placement results in more efficient utilization of light for the manufacture of sugars.

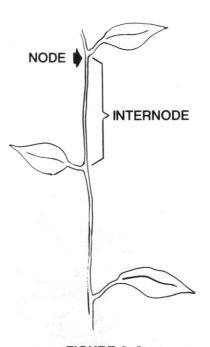

FIGURE 3–9
In low light, leaves are spaced far apart;
internodes are long and stem is thin.

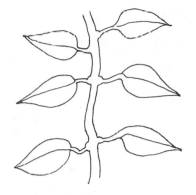

FIGURE 3–10
In high light, leaves are close together (usual distance for the species) and the stem is thick.

Table 3–6 describes the effects of electric light on plant growth.

In addition to the intensity of green observed due to light intensity, light intensity will influence the amount of red, yellow and other colors found in plants. The pigments responsible for red, purple, and blue colors need light to form. In the dark or at very low light intensities, the pigment is not formed. The amount of yellow pigment formed is also influenced by the amount of light; usually, more yellow pigment is formed under high light intensities than under low intensities. Thus, you should expect that new growth of highly colored plants will be pale; the colors will be less intense under low light conditions than when they were grown in greenhouses under optimum light intensities.

ESSENTIAL ELEMENTS AND PLANT GROWTH

All plants require 16 elements for normal and healthy growth. These come from the air and as nutrients dissolved in the water in the soil. The different elements and their sources are as follows:

From the air: Carbon (C), hydrogen (H), and oxygen (O)

From the soil: Nitrogen (N), phosphorus (P), potassium (K), calcium (Ca), magnesium (Mg), sulfur (S), iron (Fe), manganese (Mn), zinc (Zn), copper (Cu), boron (B), molybdenum (Mo), and chlorine (Cl)

TABLE 3-6
Effect of Different Types of Electric Lamps on Plant Growth

Lamp	Leaf									Stem						Side Shoots			Flowering			Comments
	Spacing			Color			Size			Rate of growth			Thickness									
	closer than normal	normal	wider than normal	light	normal	dark	small	normal	larger	slow	normal	fast	thin	normal	thick	many	average	few	over long period	normal duration	rapidly flowering	
Fluorescent, cool white, warm white		•			•			•		•				•		•			•			Leaf parallel to lamp
Fluorescent, plant-grow lamps, old	•					•			•	•					•		•					Late flowering
Fluorescent, plant-grow lamps, improved			•	•								•						•			•	Leaves reach for light

58

Lamp type								Comments
High-intensity discharge, deluxe mercury and metal halide	•	•	•	•	•	•	•	
High-intensity discharge, high-pressure sodium	•	•	•	•	•	•		Late flowering
Low-pressure sodium	•	and thicker	•	•		•	•	Some plants, e.g., African violet, impatiens, will not grow under this lamp
Incandescent and incandescent mercury	•	thinner and longer	•	•	•	•		Thick leaf rosette plants can look attractive for months before new foliage show elongated habits

Source: Adapted from H. M. Cathey and L. E. Campbell, "Interior Gardening," U.S. Department of Agriculture Home and Gardening Bulletin 220, 1978.

While all the soil elements are essential for healthy plant growth, they are not required in equal amounts. Six of the elements are required in large amounts and are known as macroelements. The older term is major elements. These are nitrogen, phosphorus, potassium, calcium, magnesium, and sulfur.

Another group of elements is required in fairly small amounts. These (iron, manganese, zinc, copper, boron, molybdenum, and chlorine) are known as microelements. Other names used in the past include minor elements and trace elements.

For each element, five zones of plant response are noted. The division between the zones is not sharp. The zones and the resulting behavior are as follows:

- **Deficient.** Plants show visual signs of the lack of the element. These are definite patterns that lead to the identification of the deficient element. General symptoms are described in Table 3–7.

- **Suboptimal.** The plant is obtaining enough of the element so that deficiency symptoms are not present. However, in this zone, plants respond to added amounts of the element.

- **Optimal.** The plant receives sufficient nutrients for optimum growth, considering the other environmental factors.

- **Supraoptimal (excess).** Like an overfed person, the plant will not respond to added amounts of the element. Growth may be slightly reduced as the level of nutrient increases.

- **Toxic.** At this very rich level, injury definitely occurs. Again, as with the deficiency, patterns are quite distinct and can be used for identification. See Table 3–8.

Putting numbers to these zones requires an understanding of the particular plant, element, and the environment. Even without numbers, the plant will tell us by its growth and appearance.

Light and Optimum Concentration.   In general, the stronger the light under which the plants are growing, the more nutrient element is needed to meet optimum requirements for plant growth. At weaker lights, overfeeding results in elongated internodes, weak stems, and poor color in the foliage. The plants will not accumulate carbohydrates for the food reserve plants need.

Soil pH and Plant Nutrition.   Soil acidity or the pH of the soil is important in determining the amount of elements available for plant

TABLE 3–7
General Symptoms of Nutrient Element Deficiency
(specific symptoms often vary from species to species)

NUTRIENT ELEMENT (SYMBOL)	SYMPTOMS
Nitrogen (N)	Small leaves, short, small, thin growth. Uniform yellowing of leaves, becoming red in severe cases. Leaf abscission occurs, beginning with older leaves.
Phosphorus (P)	Bronze to red coloration of dull-green leaves; shoots short and thin.
Potassium (K)	On older leaves, marginal chlorosis followed by marginal necrosis.
Calcium (Ca)	Death of the terminal bud, often preceded by chlorosis of the young foliage. Leaves may be distorted with the tip hooked back. Root system damaged first, usually as death of the root tips.
Magnesium (Mg)	Interveinal chlorosis on the older foliage, followed by interveinal necrosis.
Boron (B)	Distortion or thickening, or both, of the young terminal foliage. Some chlorotic spots may appear on the foliage. Terminal bud ceases development and lateral growth begins. Lateral growth soon goes through the same cycle described above.
Sulfur (S)	Uniform yellowing of new and young foliage.
Iron (Fe)	Interveinal chlorosis of the young foliage, followed by bleaching of leaf color to cream or white.
Copper (Cu)	Necrosis and white mottling of newer foliage. May result in small, linear, distorted leaves. Shoots die back.
Manganese (Mn)	Yellow chlorosis of foliage.
Molybdenum (Mo)	Linear leaf does not fully expand; color often bluish green; chlorosis and necrosis also present.
Zinc (Zn)	Small, narrow leaves in a rosettelike whorl.

Source: T. Furuta, *Environmental Plant Production and Marketing,* Cox Publishing Co., Arcadia, Calif., 1974.

growth. Generally, most nutrients are most available at a pH of from approximately 5.3 to 6.2. Above 7.0 in the alkaline range, most microelements are unavailable. Also, in the very acid range many elements are not available.

Some elements that are not essential but can cause injury to plants become available in acid pHs. Fluorine and aluminum are two that can cause injury at a pH below 6.0.

Temperature and Nutrition. Temperature influences plant nutrition in two ways. First there is the direct effect of temperature on plant growth. Second, the effect of temperature on the availability of plant nutrients must be considered. Both effects occur simultaneously, even though they can be studied separately. In practice, therefore, deciding the precise cause is difficult.

TABLE 3–8
General Symptoms of Toxicities

ELEMENTS	SYMPTOMS
Nitrogen (N)	In some plants (example, azalea), excess nitrates result in iron deficiency symptoms due to poor metabolism of iron. Ammonia toxicity results in injury and death of the root system. Yellowing of new foliage may appear.
Phosphorus (P)	Variable responses may appear, including iron or zinc deficiency due to tie-up in the soil. Chlorosis on the older foliage may appear. Chlorotic areas are irregular as contrasted to regular symptoms of potassium and magnesium deficiencies.
Boron (B)	On older leaves, chlorosis followed by necrosis at the tips of the serrations or irregularly along the leaf margin. Abscission of the foliage usually follows.
Lithium (Li)	Irregular marginal chlorosis and necrosis on the older foliage.
Manganese (Mn)	Chlorosis and yellowing of the new foliage may appear following steam sterilization due to the action of temperature above 150°F on release of free manganese in the soil. Also may appear due to highly acid conditions or poor aeration.
Aluminum (Al)	Death of the plant, usually preceded by variable chlorosis of the foliage. Usually results from highly acid conditions. Pink hydrangea flowers become blue when aluminum is present.

Source: T. Furuta, *Environmental Plant Production and Marketing,* Cox Publishing Co., Arcadia, Calif., 1974.

The direct effect of temperature is commonly observed. At very cold temperatures, the plant is killed. At somewhat warmer temperatures, only injury to some parts occurs. At still warmer temperatures, the plant grows slowly. Increasing temperature results in increased plant growth until the optimum is reached. For most plants this is somewhere between approximately 55° and 85°F. Specific plants are different optimums. Above the optimum temperature, plant growth begins to decrease. The final plant reactions as temperature increases are injury and death of the entire plant.

Plants that are growing rapidly require more nutrients than those growing slowly. The optimum concentration does not change, only a greater supply is needed over time so that the plant will maintain an optimum nutritional level.

At low soil temperatures the availability of nutrients decreases. At the same time, root growth slows or ceases. Plants may show signs of nutrient deficiency as a result. The low soil temperature may exert a direct effect on plant nutrients. Diffusion of elements out of coated particles is slowed. Movement in the soil is also slowed. When the availability of nutrients is dependent upon a microbial breakdown, as with organic fertilizers and urea formaldehydes (UF), lower soil temperatures result in lesser availability.

CHAPTER FOUR
The Interior Landscape Environment

Each interior situation will have requirements unique to itself. There will be "people" problems and problems imposed by the physical situation. Both must be considered and appropriate steps taken.

The people ordering the planting will have some level of commitment for attractive interior landscapes. Determine the amount of commitment—the peoples' plant interaction group—and plan accordingly. A high commitment may require installation of an elaborate planting and ensure a high level of maintenance with plants that may be somewhat touchy. On the other hand, if the commitment level is low, a planting of the tough plants that will look presentable without much care may be called for.

During the initial physical survey, pay particular attention to (1) light intensity, (2) location of windows and skylights, (3) type of lamps, (4) drafts from open doors, heater, or air conditioning vents, (5) planters and how

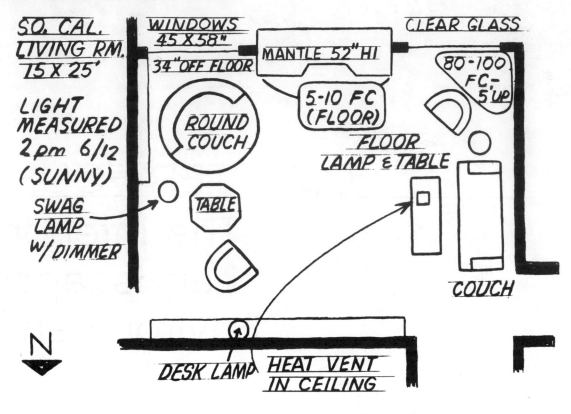

FIGURE 4–1
Sketch of room with pertinent information for interior landscaping.

they are constructed, especially drainage, and (6) benches or seats located next to or near the planters. See Figure 4–1 and Table 4–1 for guides for making the initial survey.

LIGHT

Usually considered the most difficult factor to handle, lighting raises many questions. The problem is not always too low a light intensity; situations exist where excessive light intensities do exist during part of the day. Actually, the problems associated with light are not difficult to handle. It is possible that some expense will be incurred, and it may be necessary to change the interior decoration scheme.

TABLE 4–1
Steps for Evaluation of the Interior Landscape

Step I: Sketch of room, including location of windows, doors, posts, and other structural elements that influence the use of plants. Note the location of furniture and the traffic flow of the room.

Step II: Identification of specific information on different elements in the room. This information may be placed directly on the sketch.

   A. Windows: Size
                  Type of glass used, including tinting
                  Distance from plant location
                  Direction window is facing
                  Overhang outside window
                  Louvers over window for sunlight control
                  Blinds or curtains
                  Orientation

   B. Electric lights: Type
                    Number
                    Location

   C. Heater and air-conditioning vents

   D. Skylights: Types and size
                 Types of glass or covering
                 Sunlight pattern on floor, winter and summer

   E. Doors

Step III: Measure specific environmental conditions.

   A. Light intensity: Daytime when room is occupied and lights and windows
                        set for normal operation.
                  Daytime when room is not occupied.
                  Nighttime.

   B. Temperature: Daytime when room is occupied.
                  Daytime when room is not occupied.
                  Nighttime.

   C. Humidity: same as temperature.

Step IV: Determine purpose or functional use for plants.

How to Measure Light Intensity

Plants perceive light differently from humans. To a plant, only some colors are physiologically active. Red and blue are the most active in promoting plant responses.

Most light meters are balanced to measure light as humans will see light. Humans are most aware of orange. Furthermore, humans see white light rather than the colors. Standard light meters are the only way to accurately assess the intensity of light at a given spot. They should be used. An inexpensive meter is all that is needed; the margin of error that is permissible is large indeed.

When the source of light is not sunlight, or when sunlight comes through colored window glass, the source of light and its color spectrum should be determined. In this way, one can determine if enough physiologically active colors are present to maintain healthy plants.

Light intensity should be measured at the locations where plants are to be used. For an example, see Table 4–2. It is important to know the intensity at the various levels where the tops of the plants are expected to be. The light intensity should be measured with the normal number of light bulbs; it would be risky to assume or estimate the light levels. Light coming from all directions should be measured.

Only a very few plants are tough enough to remain attractive for extended periods of time in dark areas. If the light intensity is 150 footcandles or more, it is sufficiently bright for most plants to be attractive. Unless it is desired that the plants grow normally, intensities higher than this are not needed.

When light intensities are lower than 150 footcandles, three possible courses of action are open: (1) replace the plants frequently enough so that

TABLE 4–2
Average Light Intensities at Different Locations and Plants to Use in These Locations

		Approximate Distance From (feet)		
Lighting Classifications	Average Minimum Intensity in Footcandles	Large Window	Uncovered 100-watt Bulb	Uncovered, Two 40-watt Fluorescent Bulbs
Low	25	8 or more	3	5
Medium	100	4 to 8	1.25	2.5
High	200	Less than 4 (except north-facing window)	—	1.5

the planting is attractive and the desired effect is maintained; (2) use only tough plants that will remain attractive in the low light levels, and institute a "survival only" maintenance program; and (3) install additional electrical lights to bring the intensity to desirable levels.

Selection of lamps to increase the light intensity must consider the distance from the light to the plants and the type of lamp to use. If the lights are to be placed within 3 feet of the plants, fluorescent tubes may be used. The lights need not be placed overhead; they may be placed at the side of the plants. Thus, such an arrangement may be used to backlight the planting. Because plants will "reach for the light" or all the leaves and the stem will grow in the direction of the light (this will happen, for instance, if plants are exposed to or placed by a window), the plants must be turned frequently. For this close spacing, cool white or warm white fluorescent tubes should be used because the color balance results in normal appearing plants. Where their pinkish color could be used effectively, the special plant-growing tubes may also be used.

Where several feet of space separate plants from the light source, such as in a shopping mall, high-intensity discharge lamps or low-pressure sodium lamps should be used. Another solution would be to have a bank of many high-output fluorescent tubes, but this may not be the most attractive solution or fit into the decoration scheme.

The type of plant growth one may expect from each type of light is summarized in Table 3–6. Some types of growth are not desirable from an esthetic viewpoint. Plants need red and blue light for normal-appearing growth. The color emitted by the different types of light bulbs varies; the sources mentioned previously will result in normal-appearing growth. Details are given in Table 3–6. The efficiency and life of the lamps, and all the costs of installation and operation must also be considered. The source of light is to be determined in the initial survey.

Skylights may be the source of considerable trouble, so their presence, location in relation to the planting, and whether sunlight will fall on the plants at any time during the year should be considered. The type of glass used should be determined; clear glass will transmit 85 to 90 percent of the sunlight, whereas translucent glass will reduce the amount of light transmitted to a considerable degree. If sunlight falls on the plants, the leaves will heat up and burn, especially if the plants are dry, as will be discussed under irrigation schedule. The light energy is absorbed and converted into heat.

The location of the sunlight throughout the year can be determined by knowing the orientation of the building and the height of the sun above the horizon during the various parts of the year.

If plantings must be located where sunlight will strike them during

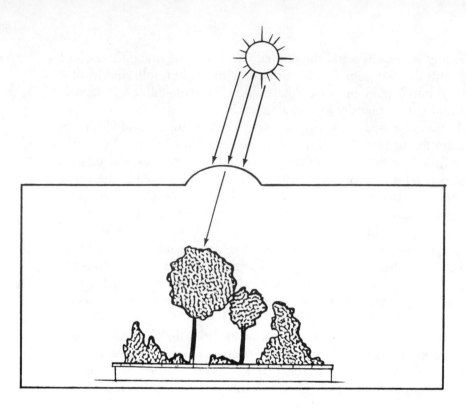

TO CORRECT

FILTER LIGHT TO
REDUCE INTENSITY

BY........

PAINT ON GLASS   TRANSLUCENT GLASS

OR   OR

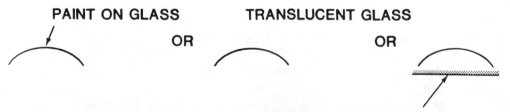

SCREEN UNDERNEATH

FIGURE 4–2
Skylights and solutions to problems.

FLUORESCENT TUBES
Number of tubes to use depends
on height. Use enough to attain
150 footcandles of light intensity on
the plants. Use high-output tubes.
Possible combinations include:
- solid cool white tubes
- solid warm white tubes
- alternate cool and warm white
  tubes
- alternate cool white and plant-
  growing tubes
- cool or warm white tubes with
  10% of wattage in
  incandescent bulbs

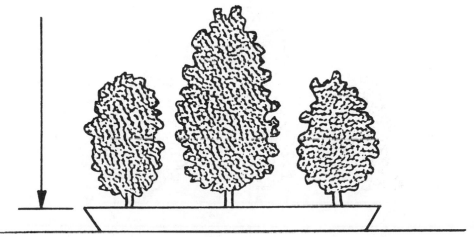

**8 FEET
OR LESS**

**FIGURE 4–3
Suggested lighting for interior plantings.**

METAL HALIDE OR HIGH-
PRESSURE SODIUM LAMPS.
If distance is excessive, such as
several floors, high-intensity lamps
such as xenon lamps may be
necessary.

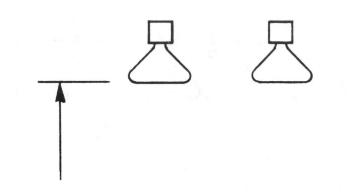

OVER 8 FEET

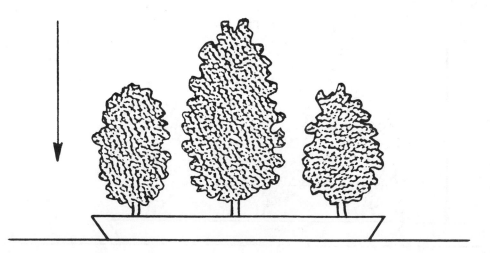

FIGURE 4–4
Suggested lighting for interior plantings.

TABLE 4–3
Approximate Light Intensities in Footcandles from Standard 40-watt, T12, Cool White Fluorescent Tubes

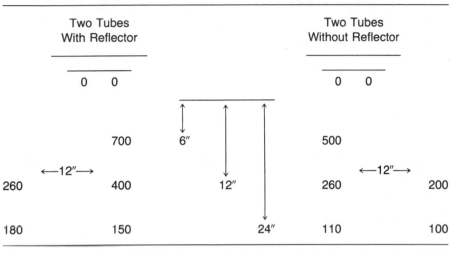

Two Tubes With Reflector			Two Tubes Without Reflector	
	0 0		0 0	
	700	6″	500	
←12″→			←12″→	
260	400	12″	260	200
180	150	24″	110	100

Source: Adapted from H. M. Cathey and L. E. Campbell, "Interior Gardening," U.S. Department of Agriculture, Home and Garden Bulletin 220, 1978.

parts of the year, steps must be taken to reduce the intensity. Cloth or paint may be used to reduce the intensity. Where permanent reduction is desired, replacing glass with translucent panels is a method to consider. Sunlight reaching the plants should not exceed 1500 footcandles.

TABLE 4–4
Relative Energy-use Efficiency and Relative Life of Some Lamps Useful for the Maintenance of Plants in Retail Displays

LAMP	LIGHT OUTPUT PER WATT	RELATIVE VALUES FOR COMPARISON OF LAMPS
Fluorescent		
cool white	1.0	1.0
warm white	1.0	1.0
plant-grow lamps	0.3 to 0.7	0.5
Discharge	0.7 to 2.0	1.5 to 2.0

Source: Adapted from H. M. Cathey and L. E. Campbell, "Interior Gardening," U.S. Department of Agriculture, Home and Garden Bulletin 220, 1978.

TABLE 4–5
Distance from the Lamp to the Plant that Results in Equal Amounts of Plant Growth

TYPE OF LAMP	APPROXIMATE DISTANCE
Fluorescent lamps, 40 watt	
cool white	15 in.
warm white	15 in.
gro-lux	10 in.
gro-lux, WS	13 in.
agro-lite	13 in.
vita-lite	13.5 in.
High-intensity discharge	
mercury	5 ft.
metal halide	7 ft.
high-pressure sodium	8 ft.
Discharge, low-pressure sodium	4.8 ft.
Incandescent	3.5 ft.
Incandescent, mercury	7 ft.

Source: Adapted from H. M. Cathey and L. E. Campbell, "Interior Gardening," U.S. Department of Agriculture Home and Gardening Bulletin 220, 1978.

Another solution where sunlight strikes interior landscapes would be to use cacti and succulents. These often can withstand the sunlight where tropical plants and other evergreens cannot. Use of cacti and succulents also leads to low-maintenance plantings. Irrigation and fertilization are given at less frequent intervals compared with tropical plants. From the design viewpoint, a contrast to the usual green interior planting is presented. This could be a welcome relief.

CONTAINERS AND PLANTERS

A container connotes a freestanding vessel in which one or more plants are placed or planted. A planter, on the other hand, implies a permanent part of the structure in which one or more plants are planted in soil or in which containers with plants are placed.

Many problems may be avoided if built-in planters are provided with adequate drainage pipes connected to the sewer system. Unfortunately, this is not always the case; either the drain is completely lacking or the pipe is much too small. If possible, especially if you are consulted before the building is constructed, be certain that adequate-sized drains are installed. The size to use will depend on the size of the planter. Figures 4–5 through 4–7 give some suggestions.

The location of clean-out plugs for the drainage system should be noted. Over time it is possible for roots to grow into the drainage system, plugging them. One way to correct a plugged drain is the use of a root cutter in the drain pipe. If each planter has a clean-out plug, the operation becomes a simple one. If such plugs were not installed during construction, suitable clean-out plugs should be installed in the planter.

Furthermore, water traps should be installed in the drainage system from each planter. This will prevent odorous to toxic gases from coming back into the planter from the sewer system.

Many shopping malls and other buildings leave "holes in the floor" into which plants are to be placed. Because the ground under the building has been compacted before it was built, drainage through the soil from these planters is usually poor to nonexistent unless soil is removed to a level below the compacted soil. A few test holes will tell you how deep

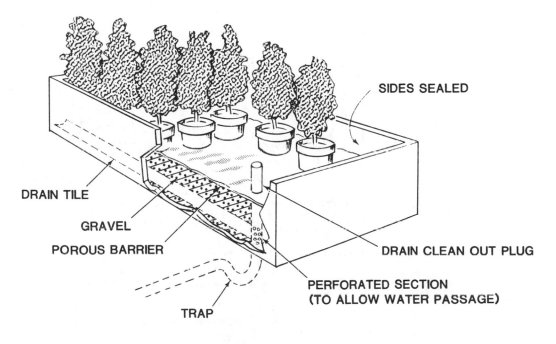

FIGURE 4–5
Suggested installation of plants in a large
planter.

this is. After excavation, the infiltration rate of the soil should be determined; this will indicate how much water can be expected to drain away in a given period of time. If the infiltration is very low, one or more sumps should be installed; these are holes drilled several feet into the soil and then filled with rock. A screen over the top will prevent soil from infiltrating and plugging the sump.

Following the preparation of the bottom, the sides should be sealed with several layers of water-soluble asphalt so that water will not seep under the floor to cause problems.

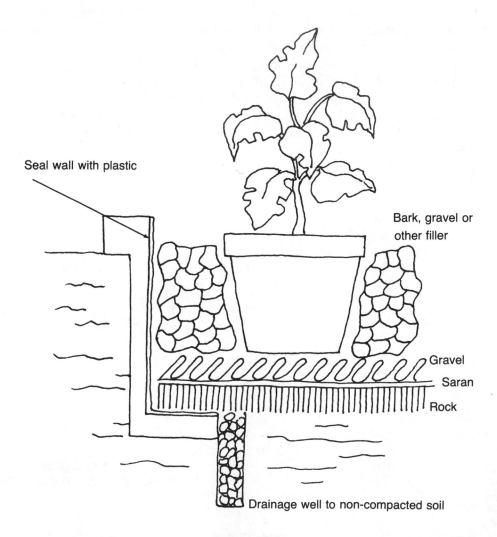

FIGURE 4–6
Planters on grade.

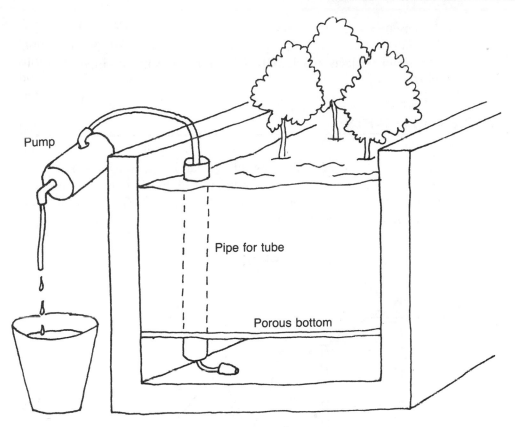

Pump

Pipe for tube

Porous bottom

FIGURE 4–7
Planter without drainage. Suggestions on
installation to remove drainage water.

A layer of rock should be placed on the bottom of the planter and then
the planting installed. It is often desirable to place containers with plants
into the planter and maintain the planting in this manner. Leaving plants
in their original containers permits the following: (1) removal of a single
plant and replacement without disturbing any of the other plants, (2) separate irrigation and fertilization practices for plants, and (3) better control
of excess water so that drainage is kept to a minimum.

BENCHES AND SEATS NEAR PLANTINGS

Benches are often included as part of the grouping where plants are used.
This is desirable. However, you should be aware that raised planters are
often a tempting object upon which to sit, at least on the sides, and that

in the absence of benches, people will do so. This could result in injury to the plants or in trash in the planter. It could also result in the placing of undesirable objects and liquids on or into the soil in which plants are growing.

VENTILATION AND DRAFTS

A very common problem faced by interior landscape designers and maintenance personnel is the proper handling of drafts. Usually, the problem is from heating and air-conditioning vents, but drafts from outside doors and windows must also be considered.

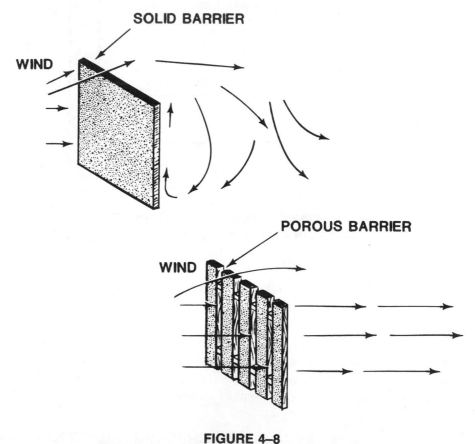

FIGURE 4–8
Influence of type of windbreak on air movement.
(Source: E. B. Moysey, and F. B. McPherson,
"Effect of Porosity on Performance of
Windbreaks," _Trans. Amer. Soc. Agr. Eng._ 9:74–
76, 1966.)

WINDBREAK POROSITY

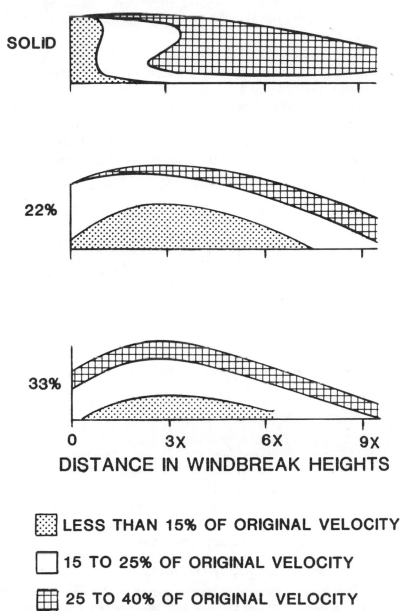

SOLID

22%

33%

0   3X   6X   9X

DISTANCE IN WINDBREAK HEIGHTS

LESS THAN 15% OF ORIGINAL VELOCITY

15 TO 25% OF ORIGINAL VELOCITY

25 TO 40% OF ORIGINAL VELOCITY

FIGURE 4–9
Influence of porosity of windbreak on wind speed
as a percentage of original velocity. (Adapted
from E. B. Moysey, and F. B. McPherson, "Effect
of Porosity on Performance of Windbreaks,"
Trans. Amer. Soc. Agr. Eng. 9:74–76, 1966.)

Two types of problems may arise. First, plants may dry out to the point of injury because of the dessicating effect of air blasts. Second, the plant may suffer chilling injury. Many tropical plants are injured when the air temperature reaches 40° to 45°F.

Plants should not be placed against vents. It may be possible to adjust the air deflectors in a manner to keep the air drafts off the plants and still have uniform temperatures in the room.

The final solution would be to place interior windbreaks between the opening and the planting. Wind baffles will deflect the wind and give protection for up to five to eight times their height. The most effective baffles are rather porous; 25 to 40 percent of the area should be open.

AIR POLLUTION

Unfortunately, in most urban areas air pollution is a fact of life. Even in many of the more rural areas, air pollution will be an important consideration at times. Therefore, the designer and maintainer of indoor land-

TABLE 4–6
Generalized Symptoms of Air Pollutants on Plants

POLLUTANT	SYMPTOMS (GENERALIZED)
Sulfur dioxide	Irregular spots turning white or tan along the margin and between the veins of broadleaf plants. Tips brown with handling bordered by a chlorotic zone.
Ethylene	Epinasty or abscission or death of leaves without chlorosis. Excess branching may occur. Blossom may abscise or fail to develop normally.
Ozone	Upper surface of the leaves of broadleaved plants stippled or flecked with small, irregular areas with red-brown or straw to white color.
PAN (Oxidant smog) (peroxyacetyl nitrate)	Silvering to bronze underside of young foliage. Often banded zones in leaf, especially on grasses. On conifers, needle blight with some chlorosis.
Fluorides	Burned tips or edges or both of leaf with separation between dead and living tissue sharp.

Source: T. Furuta, *Environmental Plant Production and Marketing.* Cox Publishing Co., Arcadia, Calif., 1974.

scapes should remember that air pollutants may cause injury from time to time. See Table 4–6.

Most air-conditioning and air-handling systems for buildings do not reduce or eliminate air pollutants. If interior air is recirculated and no outside fresh air is admitted, the level of some pollutants such as PANs will be reduced. Activated charcoal filters may be used to reduce or eliminate air pollutants. They are expensive and maintenance costs are high.

With the emphasis on saving energy, many buildings are sealed more tightly. Infiltration of outside air is reduced, thus conserving energy. However, air pollutants from indoor sources are not diluted. Consequently, they accumulate and can become harmful to plants. Cases where human discomfort has increased have been cited.

CHAPTER FIVE
Horticultural Considerations Before Installation

Ultimately, the attractiveness and usefulness of interior landscapes will depend upon the knowledge and skill of the horticulturists that take care of the plantings and will be consulted in regard to the plantings. More than any one separate group, the horticulturist will blend the knowledge of science and art together in the social context of the interior landscape. His or her skill will be evident to all that come into that environment.

The need for horticultural skills occurs long before a specific interior receives plants and long before the plants are cared for in that environment. Expertly grown plants must be secured. The plants must be properly grown, conditioned, and shaped to fulfill their function in the interior landscape. Because the interior landscape is more demanding and less forgiving of error than exterior landscapes, and because all plants are usually observed at close range in the interior, only excellent plants will give the desired results. Thus, the horticulturist growing plants for interior use must shape the plants, provide the proper soil mixtures, or the proper water–soil–fertilizer system, and properly condition the plants to withstand interior conditions and environments. The designer who attempts to use just any plant in an interior is doing a disservice to the clients, because the plants will fail, and no amount of skill in managing the plants will overcome the use of improperly prepared and grown plants.

Thus, horticultural skills are needed in the design phase. Are the plants properly prepared and grown? Will the containers and other planting situations be adequate with regard to environment, soil, drainage, air circulation, drafts, and so on? The choice of shape, color, texture and other considerations of design are essentially esthetic and artistic decisions. The choice of plants, soil mixtures, fertilizer systems, and the like are horticultural decisions and will determine whether the artistic solutions to the interior landscape problems will be adequate.

The actual installation of the interior landscape requires extensive knowledge of horticulture to be certain that the plants are properly planted. The exact positioning of the plant will be a design or artistic decision, but horticultural requirements cannot be neglected, because skylights, drafts, and electrical lights may necessitate modification of the plan during the installation phase. For example, plants cannot be positioned under clear glass skylights because leaf injury will occur due to the heating effect when sunlight falls directly on them. The plants must be moved out of the sunlight or a translucent cover placed on the skylight.

During the installation of the interior landscape, the actual planting must be carefully done. The roots of the plants should be pruned and the soil properly packed. Consideration must also be given to the possibility of placing the plants into location without removing them from the containers in which they grew. This increases maintenance considerations because each plant must be irrigated separately as they are living in separate containers. However, there are advantages to such plantings.

Improper maintenance of interior plantings can negate all the efforts and expense that have gone before. Here a great deal of horticultural knowledge and a liberal dose of common sense are needed. At times the horticulturist must be a detective to determine the cause of problems and other times, a counselor. Whatever the role, the maintenance of the interior planting requires flexibility and knowledge.

SOIL MIXTURE

Foliage plants will adapt to and grow well in a wide variety of soil mixtures. A good soil mixture for plants in interior landscapes is one that holds enough water to maintain life, yet has enough pore space so that, when the soil is wet, enough oxygen reaches the roots. See Figure 5–1. Then, for practical purposes, the soil mixture must not weigh too much.

Soil mixtures may be described in terms of their composition, that is, the amount of each ingredient used. An example is one part peat moss and one part perlite. Another is one part bark, one part peat moss, and one part perlite. Both of these soil mixtures are widely used in interior landscapes. Because the ingredients have consistence in properties, the properties of the resulting mix are consistent from batch to batch. Thus, other cultural practices may be continued in the same manner without danger of harm.

Soil mixtures may also be described in terms of physical and chemical properties. The usual properties of importance are bulk density or weight of the soil, water-holding capacity, air-filled porosity, pH, and cation-exchange capacity. It is probably best to describe soil mixtures by these properties, with the ingredients also specified. Then the user may be cer-

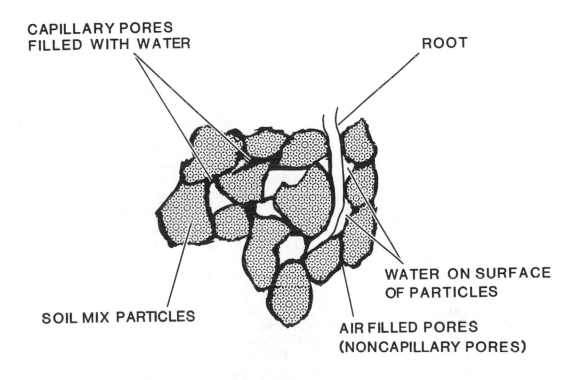

CAPILLARY PORES
FILLED WITH WATER

ROOT

WATER ON SURFACE
OF PARTICLES

SOIL MIX PARTICLES

AIR FILLED PORES
(NONCAPILLARY PORES)

FIGURE 5–1
Enlarged schematic of soil mixture showing
major components.

TABLE 5–1
Soil Amendments and Their Characteristics

TYPE OF AMENDMENT	REMARKS
Sand	Seldom used alone because of increase in density, reduced aeration, etc. Often used in combination with organic matter. A relatively coarse sand should be used. As the mineral part of a UC mixture, the sand should be fine. Low cation-exchange capacity.
Vermiculite	High cation-exchange capacity, but will not stand compaction when wet. Decreases bulk density. Increases moisture-holding capacity. Should be used only in combination with organic amendments.
Perlite	Lightweight mineral product with low cation-exchange and water-holding capacity. Increases aeration and reduces bulk density.
Calcined clay	Variable product depending on manufacturer. Increases bulk density. Often low cation-exchange and moisture-holding capacity. Product will increase aeration. May contain excess salts.
Sawdust, various	Requires additional nitrogen for decomposition. Rate of decomposition variable depending on species. Material widely used for soil amendment. Low cation-exchange capacity. May contain substances toxic to plant growth. Sawdust that decomposes rapidly, like that of shortleaf pine, requires large initial amounts of N; there usually is a sudden release of N as the sawdust becomes essentially broken down, which may injure the plants. Alternative as fuel, so cost may be a factor. Availability also a consideration.
Peat moss	Variable product depending on origin. Sphagnum peat excellent for soil mixtures. High cation-exchange capacity and moisture retention. Coarse ground product should be used. Peat may contain weed seeds and excessive soluble salts.
Manures	Often contain excessive amounts of salts and must be thoroughly leached. Product usually variable with time, resulting in poor consistency and reproducibility of soil mixtures.
Bark	Excellent where it is available. An alternative use is as fuel.

tain that cultural practices need not be altered. Suggested standards for soil mix properties are given in Table 5–2.

Bulk density is simply the weight of a given volume of soil. It may be expressed as pounds per cubic foot or grams per 100 cubic centimeters. Bulk density may be expressed as wet or dry soil. The wet weight is the preferred value because the designer then knows the weight to plan for; many plants can add considerable weight for the floor to bear.

Water-holding capacity is simply the ability of the soil mixture to hold water. Generally, the more water the soil holds, the longer will be the interval between irrigations. By knowing this value and the amount of water used by the plant on a daily basis, the horticulturist can predict the interval between irrigations. Practically, maintenance companies want soil mixtures that will hold enough water for the plant between visits of their personnel.

Air-filled porosity is that space in the soil where air will be found following irrigation and drainage. Roots need air to function properly. If the amount of air is inadequate, many forms of abnormal growth, from distorted leaves to plant death, will be seen.

The *soil pH* is important because the availability of plant nutrients varies with pH. The pH may change depending on the water and the fertilizers used. Frequent tests should be made to be certain the pH remains in the desired range.

Cation-exchange capacity is a measure of the soil's ability to retain nutrients. Horticulturally, this is not as critical a property as some of the others. Controlled-release fertilizers and frequent applications of fertilizer may be used to maintain adequate nutrient levels. However, this capacity helps to maintain a reserve nutrient supply. All of the cation-exchange capacity in the typical mixture for interior plants will come from the organic matter being used.

TABLE 5–2
Suggested Standards for Soil Mixture for Interior Landscapes

Physical Properties	
Bulk density	0.6 to 1.2 grams per cubic centimeter wet weight
Water-holding capacity	20% to 60% by volume
Air-filled porosity	Minimum 15% after water drains
Chemical Characteristics	
pH	5.5 to 6.5
Cation-exchange capacity	30 milliequivalents per 100 cubic centimeters

The function of the soil mixture is to support the plant, to provide water for life and growth and to contain a reservoir of nutrients needed for plant growth. Unless the interior environment is unusually bright, the kind of plant growth that occurs will not be very attractive; therefore, in most situations, growth should not be forced on plants. Slow growth means, from a practical viewpoint, that the amount of water and nutrients (fertilizer) required is greatly reduced. Fertilizer, therefore, is applied infrequently, usually not more than once every three months.

The amount of pore space, the water-holding capacity, and the rate the plant uses water influence the irrigation frequency of plants in interior landscapes. These factors are covered in more detail under the section on irrigation. Water is applied when the soil becomes dry; you can tell dryness by feeling the soil and observing the plants. At each irrigation, sufficient amounts of water are applied to thoroughly wet the soil mass and allow some to drain away.

HYDROPONICS

Most of the plants used in containers for interior landscape are growing in soil mixtures especially formulated for container use. The soil is porous, infiltrates water rapidly, and drains rapidly. At the same time, when the soil mixture is wet, the number of large pores are sufficient to provide excellent aeration. The mixtures are also formulated so that they are not excessively heavy.

If the preceding is true, and it is in many cases, why do many persons have such difficult times in keeping interior landscapes healthy and attractive? Probably the reasons revolve around considerations such as not appreciating the differences in the handling requirements of different soil mixtures, that is, not learning to handle each type of soil mixture so as to be certain when the soil is dry, when it is moist, how much fertilizer is needed, and how much water is needed at each irrigation. All these are considerations that cause problems; thus, if a grouping has plants growing in several types of soil (different soil mixtures), treating all alike could cause problems.

This is not to say that you cannot learn to do the necessary task of maintaining excellent interior plantings growing in soil. The number of excellent plantings attests to the fact that people have learned to do so; it takes common sense, which all of us possess.

In an attempt to simplify maintenance problems and perhaps as a means of gaining market advantages with a different system, hydroponics have been developed. In some countries this type of system for interior plantings has gained much favor. These systems of culture simplify the irrigation and fertilization requirements, but they also present some problems not found in soil systems.

Hydroponics has come to mean all the procedures and systems that permit the culture of plants without the use of a soil or a soil mixture. Water and necessary nutrients are provided, and the plant is supported by mechanical means in some cases.

Several general classes of systems can be distinguished. All have many modifications to permit their use in almost every situation where plants are being grown. These modifications also permit use of the systems in small-scale applications, such as one container for the desk, or in many acres of commercial production.

The principal classes of systems are outlined in Table 5–3. Because specific specifications depend on the location, the designer should understand the possibilities and seek qualified consultants for each specific application.

Small-scale gravel culture procedures have found much favor for interior landscapes. The system is not complicated, requires no external power, and is not dependent on the use of motors and pumps for correct operation. The simple replacement of water and nutrients with periodic flushing of the system is all that is required.

Containers are designed so that a portion of the bottom rests in water or water plus fertilizer. Water rises by capillarity throughout the growing

TABLE 5–3
Principal Fertilization Procedures for Hydroponics

Liquid	Maintain a solution of fertilizer in water. Several formulas have been proposed. All have been used successfully. Solution should be changed frequently to maintain proper fertility level.
Exchange resin	Some resins with nutrient elements adhering to the surface have been used. The resins must be replaced on a regular basis as the nutrients are used. Resins are usually placed in the water reservoir.
Coated fertilizer	A coated fertilizer may be used for long-term fertilization of hydroponic systems. The fertilizer particles may be incorporated in the growing medium or may be placed in the reservoir water. Replacement of the fertilizer on a periodic basis is needed. One of the coated fertilizers that has been useful is sold under the trade name of Osmocote®. Several formulations are available, so specific information should be developed for each location.

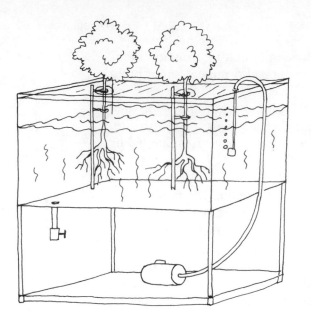

TANK. Tank is a container filled with solution. Air is bubbled into solution to maintain favorable oxygen level in solution. Plants must have artificial support.

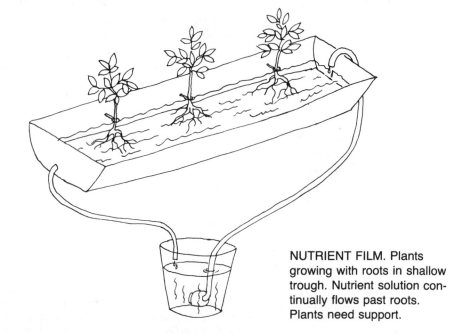

NUTRIENT FILM. Plants growing with roots in shallow trough. Nutrient solution continually flows past roots. Plants need support.

(a) Water culture: Roots growing in a nutrient solution.

FIGURE 5–2
Hydroponic systems that can be adapted for interior landscapes.

SMALL CONTAINER. Container sets in layer of nutrient solution. Water by capillary pull.

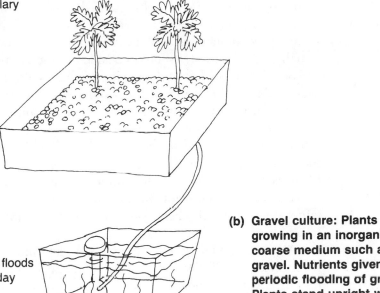

LARGE SCALE. Pump floods gravel at least once a day with nutrient solution.

(b) Gravel culture: Plants growing in an inorganic coarse medium such as gravel. Nutrients given by periodic flooding of gravel. Plants stand upright without support.

(c) Sand: Fine, wet medium such as sand. Nutrient solution drips onto sand. Plants do not need artificial support. Continuous flow of solution maintained.

FIGURE 5–2 (Continued)

medium, thereby supplying the needed moisture. All one needs to do is maintain the proper water level in the reservoir. Usually, an indicator or meter is incorporated as a part of the container or as a separate device to visually tell when water should be added to the reservoir.

Soil is not used for the growing of the plants. Rather, a porous clay aggregate is used for most systems; some systems depend on the use of vermiculite. It would be possible to use other nonsoil aggregates.

Fertilization has been generally done by dissolving fertilizer in the water that is contained in the reservoir. One system utilizes fertilizer elements attached to ion-exchange resins. Either way, the application of fertilizer is simple; following a few simple steps is all that is needed.

The roots of the plant will grow out of the drainage hole of the container holding the clay aggregate. This is not harmful and should not lead to problems.

Algae can and do grow in the medium and in the reservoir. This must be cleaned periodically; the usual recommendation is to wash the reservoir monthly. Under some situations this can be a difficult task to accomplish.

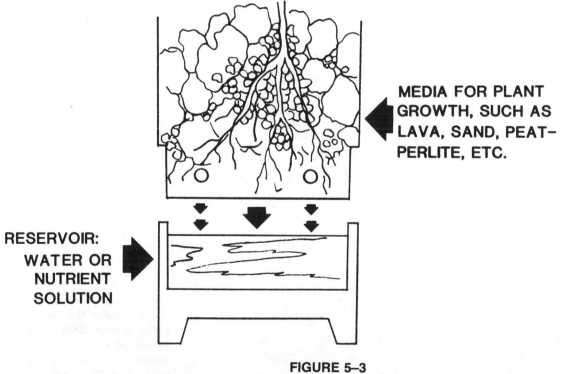

MEDIA FOR PLANT GROWTH, SUCH AS LAVA, SAND, PEAT-PERLITE, ETC.

RESERVOIR: WATER OR NUTRIENT SOLUTION

FIGURE 5–3
Planter for hydroponic growing of foliage plants for interior landscape.

Controlling the "dryness" of the medium will be difficult. The systems are designed for the plants to have a constant source of water, never going without in a dry soil. Thus, plants will grow, and the growth occurring in interior conditions, particularly where the light conditions are unfavorable, is usually very unattractive.

All plant species have not adapted well to this procedure. No doubt future improvements will lead to their successful growth in hydroponic systems.

Finally, transporting plants growing in these aggregates is not trouble free. Constant shaking of the container will cause aggregates to rub against roots and stems, injuring them to the point where disease and death may occur.

Despite the problems, hydroponic systems for interior landscapes will be utilized more and more. Technical improvements may overcome many of the problems cited.

PROPERLY CONDITIONED PLANTS

Properly conditioned plants are those that, when placed into interior landscapes, will not lose leaves and will be attractive. Improperly conditioned plants may drop all leaves and will appear unattractive until new leaves develop. Leaf drop is the result of any of three factors: (1) Leaves developing in high-light conditions fall when placed in low-light conditions. (2) Leaves lacking water will fall. This condition may be caused by withholding water or by cutting the roots during transplanting. (3) Soil conditions such as salinity will inhibit absorption of sufficient amounts of water.

Plants cannot be moved directly from humid, high-light conditions (outdoors, greenhouses or shadehouses) to the much dryer and darker interior conditions without the plants showing the effects of such change. This is the result of the types of leaves that are produced under the differing types of light conditions. Under high-light conditions, the plant will produce "sun leaves," relatively thick, normal, green leaves. These leaves will not change to the type that are adaptable to dark conditions, for "shade leaves" are thin, usually larger, and often darker green in color.

When sun leaves are placed in dark light conditions (low light intensity), they deteriorate, turning yellow and abscising from the plant. Many plants will show this effect—ficus, dracaena, even flowering plants such as poinsettia. On the other hand, shade leaves exposed to high light intensity can and do burn; that is, the cells are killed.

Proper conditioning requires that the plant be in low light intensities (1500 footcandles or less) for new leaves to develop in the most proper form and for the older leaves to adapt to low light. This may take as long as 8 weeks to 3 months. Thus, it is usually better to use plants that have been produced under light conditions conducive to the proper type of leaf formation.

Proper conditioning for interior plantings must also consider the plant's ability to withstand the dry interior air. Plants can be conditioned to this aspect by gradually adapting the plant, over a period of a week or more, to dryer and dryer air and soil conditions. In a greenhouse, plants recently received from growers should be misted. At first the misting of the leaves should be done very frequently, say every hour. Every day, the frequency of misting is reduced so that after 1 week to 10 days the greenhouse is no longer misted. All throughout this time, the greenhouse atmosphere should be kept dry.

At the same time that the plant tops are hardened to interior conditions, the frequency of irrigation should be reduced so that the plants become adapted to dry soil conditions. Sudden change to dry will cause all the leaves to fall. At first, the plant will be irrigated when the soil surface just begins to dry out. Then, each succeeding irrigation is given only after the soil becomes dryer—the surface is dry, then the soil dries for ½ inch, and so on. Soon, irrigation is given only after the top ¾ inch or so of the soil is dry. This is the dryness at which plants indoors will be irrigated. The only way to tell when the time to irrigate arrives is to feel the moistness of the soil. The rule to follow when in doubt about the need for irrigation is to wait overnight.

PROPERLY ESTABLISHED PLANTS

Many times problems with interior landscapes may be traced directly to plants not being established in the container for placement in the interior. Too often the plants are dug from field situations and transplanted into the interior. Unless the environment is conducive to good growth, and most interior conditions are not, the roots will not grow and become established, and death of the plants may result. The problem is particularly severe when the roots are cut and the plants are planted into larger containers or planters.

This problem can be alleviated by not disturbing the root system, or as little as possible. In larger planters, the entire container in which the plant is growing should be submerged in a medium such as gravel or peat moss. Use of soil would be the last choice unless one expects the container to eventually deteriorate and the plant to become established in the soil.

TABLE 5–4
Steps to Properly Prepare Plants for Interior Landscapes

Step 1	Remove all surface mulches, fertilizers, etc.
Step 2	Leach soil by repeated applications of water, allowing excess water to drain freely from soil.
Step 3	Place plant where light intensity will not exceed 1500 footcandles at the brightest time (noon).
Step 4	Grow plants until new leaves have developed. Irrigation must be adjusted to plant; never overwater, never irrigate on a regular schedule. Irrigate when soil becomes dry. Initially, do not fertilize. After leaves develop, fertilize infrequently to maintain healthy growth and color. Solution containing 25 ppm N once a month may be sufficient.
Step 5	Maintain attractive plant with proper irrigation and fertilizer schedule: irrigate when soil feels dry and fertilize once a month with 25 ppm N, using a fertilizer ratio of 1–1–1 or 3–1–2, for nitrogen, phosphorus, and potash. Minor elements should be applied every 6 months.

ROOTS PLUGGING DRAINAGE

The tops and roots of the plants grow slowly in interior locations. Eventually, the roots will grow into the drainage pipes and over time will become large enough to stop drainage. When this happens, of course, water will collect in the planter, causing waterlogged conditions.

This condition can be delayed by placing barriers containing copper that will permit the passage of water and slow the growth of roots between the plants and the drainage system. Unfortunately, nothing will prevent growth of roots into the drainage completely, because the only way of controlling the roots is with a solid barrier, and these will not permit drainage of excess water.

The possible actions to be taken are to periodically lift the plants in their original container and trim the roots. It is also possible that, during the building construction or plant installation phase, clean-out plugs for the drainage system can be installed. From time to time, rotating root cutters can be used in the drainage system to clear away the roots growing in them.

CHAPTER SIX
Principles of Interior Landscape Maintenance

INTRODUCTION

No matter how skilled the horticulturist growing plants for interior land-scapes, no matter how beautiful and functional the design, no matter how skillfully the interior landscape was installed, it is in the hands of the maintenance personnel to bring the planting to its ultimate beauty and utility. Unskillful handling and neglect will undo all the skills and talent exhibited in a very short period of time, even in as short a period as a couple of weeks.

The proper maintenance of interior landscapes is not difficult. Knowl-edge of the basis for plant growth and horticultural knowledge about the interaction of environmental factors are important. Of utmost importance, however, is the ability of the individuals to be observant of the story the plant is telling, to be able to decipher the symptoms, and then to act accordingly.

WHAT RESIDENTS SHOULD
AND SHOULD NOT DO

Varied reactions from the residents of the office building are to be expected. The reaction can range from actual dislike for the plants to a motherly, protective feeling (such persons know much more than the maintenance people who, they feel, are totally ignorant and inexperienced). These feelings exist because of inherent differences in peoples' need for and appreciation of plants. Discuss this with the management of the establishment, because some actions of the residents could materially affect the long-term appearance of the plantings.

Probably the two most troublesome problems associated with residents' reaction and action to plantings are (1) giving the plants too much "care," such as watering too frequently or improperly, and (2) carelessly and unthinkingly putting trash or liquids into the planting. And some people will deliberately injure plants.

Many people imagine that they know how to take care of plants; as a result, they will complain that maintenance is overwatering, underwatering, giving the incorrect amount of water, not fertilizing as frequently as necessary, or fertilizing too frequently. Whatever is done is probably wrong for these people. Establish a policy with the management of the organization that maintenance is totally responsible and will assume the blame for anything that goes wrong, provided that the residents do not attempt to care for the planting. Some reaction from residents who "know better than you" will occur. Maintenance can learn from them if they are allowed to give counsel and to help. Value their counsel, but be certain maintenance is not responsible for the injury they may cause because of overwatering, overfertilization, or whatever.

Carelessly or unthinkingly putting liquids into the container is a problem that may be difficult to prevent. Many people think of planters as convenient receptacles for trash. Why go to the restroom or coffee room to pour out unwanted coffee; put it into the soil around the plants. It is not healthy for plants to be so treated. Management must be aware of this and take steps to correct the situation; it may require the removal of plants from areas where this hazard is high.

Paper, cigarette butts, and other trash are unsightly, but they generally do not harm plants. Assume that these items will be regularly removed from the planters by the janitorial service.

Determining the number and type of plants to be used in a particular location may present problems. Some people may want many plants, more than management gives them. Others will want fewer. The best approach would be to confer with the management and the residents before making a decision on types and numbers of plants. If some flowering plants are to be used, determine allergic reactions of the residents if possible. If someone is allergic to chrysanthemums, for example, do not use these where the person can come in contact with them. Suitable substitutions are always possible.

The number of plants to be used will be the decision of management. Unless a carte blanche contract exists, it is management's decision as to where to use plants, the number involved, and the sizes. These factors affect the amount of rent charged. Be certain the company gets all they contract for, but surely do not put in more than contracted.

In approaching the problems associated with interior landscapes caused by people or residents in the building, a good measure of common sense will go a long way toward avoiding problems and solving difficulties. Flexibility and understanding of human reactions are essential. Everyone is not equally enamored of plants, and many people think they actually may know more about caring for plants than professionals.

NOT A GROWING ROOM

Conditions in buildings are usually not conducive to good plant growth. Light intensities are usually not sufficiently high. Exceptions will be found, such as African violets that grow well in low light intensities. The philosophy that full-sized or near full-sized plants should be installed, and that the maintenance program will be to keep the plants alive and looking attractive, but not rapidly growing, is a wise course to take.

LIGHTS

Light Intensity

Light intensity provides the key to determining the maintenance program as well as the selection of plants to be used. In general, the higher the light intensity, the more one may impose irrigation and fertilization programs approaching those practiced in greenhouses and other locations where plants are grown. Conversely, the lower the light intensity, the less frequent will be irrigation and fertilization, because less water and fertilizer are needed on a daily basis. Also, plant growth is controlled by reducing the available water supply. The type of growth at low light intensities will not be desirable or visually pleasing.

TABLE 6–1
Maintenance Program for Interior Landscapes Based on Light Intensity

APPROXIMATE RANGE OF LIGHT INTENSITY	MAINTENANCE PROGRAM AND COMMENTS
3000 ↑ | 800 to	Normal plant growth possible. Irrigate and fertilize regularly and frequently. Pruning needed on a regular basis to maintain proper size and appearance. Reduced irrigation frequency and fertilization will slow growth, but one must be careful plant does not suffer.
1000 ↑ 150 to	Plant growth will be slow. Irrigate only after soil approaches dryness. Reduce fertilizer dosage. Infrequent pruning will be needed.
200 ↑ | Total darkness	Do not force plant growth. Install plants at or very close to ultimate size desired. Irrigate only after soil is nearly dry. Reduce fertilizer dosage. Pruning will not be needed. Replace plants when they become unattractive.

These general remarks must be tempered by consideration of the plant species, in that the necessary light intensity will differ with plant species. Some species will survive in very low light conditions; others will not. Table 6–1 is a suggested strategy for the maintenance of interior plantings depending upon light intensity received by the plants.

Duration

Often the location where plants are located is kept rather dark, that is, light intensity is below minimum levels for good plant survival, because of the decor or mood to be created. In such a location, supplemental electrical lights are necessary to ensure healthy plants. However, the use of these lights during the time customers are around is not desirable. In such situations, higher-intensity lights should be used when people are not present.

The time of day or night that the lights are used is not important. Plants will adapt. There is, however, a correlation between duration and intensity. Within reason, brighter lights (i.e., higher intensities) are used for shorter durations. The plants do well when bright lights are used for short periods of time or dim lights are used for long periods of time. Some experts suggest that the value 2400 be used; this value is obtained by multiplying light intensity in footcandles by the hours the lights are on. Thus, if you have two of the three values, you can determine the missing value for planning purposes: light intensity in footcandles (LI) × hours of lighting (H) = 2400.

SOIL FERTILITY

Because of the low light intensities in interior situations, plants should receive only a small amount of fertilizer. The actual amount depends on the plant species and the light intensity. See Figure 6–1. The relationship of the lower the light intensity the lower the amount of fertilizer applies. Tables 6–2 and 6–3 outline fertilizer types and fertilizer programs.

Low amounts of fertilizer mean low, continuous supplies. Feast and starvation, that is, liberal or light amounts followed by fertilizer, should be avoided as much as possible.

Two fertilizer systems seem to be the most adapted for interior situations, liquid fertilizer and long-term, controlled-release fertilizer. Either can be used alone or, in unusually bright conditions, a combination may be used.

Liquid fertilizer systems use soluble fertilizer. A dilute fertilizer solution may be applied at each irrigation, or a somewhat stronger solution may be applied periodically. Normal irrigation practices are followed. Procedures are given in Tables 6–4 and 6–5 for liquid fertilizers and in Tables 6–6 and 6–7 for dry and controlled-release fertilizers.

TABLE 6–2
Definitions of Various Types of Fertilizers

FERTILIZER TYPE	DEFINITION
Controlled or slow release	Fertilizer elements become available for plant growth over an extended time.
Organic	From plant or animal sources.
Liquid	Fertilizer nutrient elements completely dissolved in water, whatever their source.
Chelated	Fertilizer nutrient element is part of a complex molecule that keeps element available for plant growth.
Dry	Fertilizers applied without dissolving in water.

TABLE 6–3
Fertilizer Programs for Interior Landscapes

APPLICATION METHOD	METHOD	ELEMENT	OBJECTIVE	COMMENTS
Preplant Incorporation	Fertilizer mixed into soil	Mg, N, K	Provide starter amounts and reserve	Use controlled-release nitrogen source
		Cu, Zn, Ca	Mix element into root system area when surface application does not move into soil	Use chelated micronutrients, and calcium sulfate
		Ca	Correct low pH	Use both hydrated lime for quick response and calcium carbonate or dolomite for lasting effect
		Fe, Mn, B	Provide reserve	Use chelated products where available; not all elements may be needed—check to be certain

APPLICATION METHOD	METHOD	ELEMENT	OBJECTIVE	COMMENTS
Postplant Liquid	Fertilizer dissolved in water and applied at periodic intervals	All	Supply essential nutrients as required by plant growth	
Constant	Fertilizer dissolved in water and applied each irrigation	All	Supply essential nutrients as needed by plants	Completely automated procedure possible
Foliar	Nutrient element sprayed on foliage	N, Fe, Mn, Mg, Cu, Zn, Mo	Quick response or when soil conditions unfavorable for absorption	Not all essential elements are absorbed by the foliage; absorption usually limited; foliar injury can occur with strong solutions
Dry; includes controlled release	Dry fertilizer applied to soil surface	All	Supply essential elements with insoluble fertilizers	Slow method of application to individual containers
Slurry	Insoluble fertilizer suspended in water and this liquid applied to soil surface	All	Speed application of insoluble materials such as organic fertilizers	

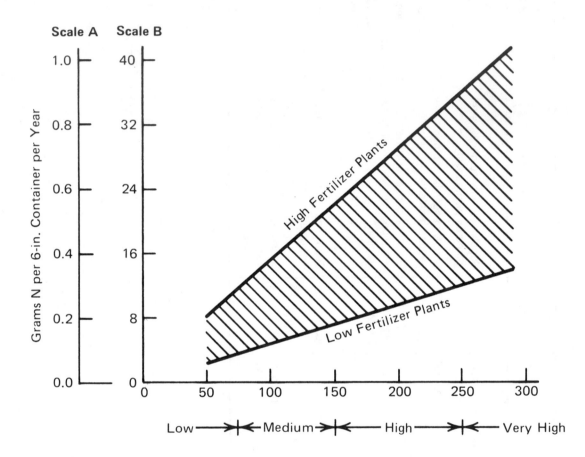

Scale A
Dry fertilizer, liquid fertilizer periodic application

Scale B
ppm N in liquid feed, constant fertilization

Light Intensity (footcandles)

FIGURE 6–1
Suggested fertilizer rates for plants in interior landscapes. Low-fertilizer plants are fleshy plants such as peperomia and other slow-growing plants, such as some ferns. High-fertilizer plants are large-leaved or rapid-growing plants such as *Ficus* and *Brassaia* (Schefflera).

TABLE 6–4
Liquid Fertilization: Determining the Concentration of Fertilizer Solution

To obtain fertilizer solutions containing definite concentrations of nutrient elements in parts per million (ppm), use the following formula: The ounces of fertilizer to dissolve in 100 gallons of water (FS) to make up the fertilizer solution is equal to the desired concentration in parts per million (DC) divided by the percentage of the element in the fertilizer used (%), multiplied by 75.

$$\frac{DC}{\% \times 75} = FS$$

If a fertilizer proportioner is to be used, the amount of fertilizer to dissolve in water for the stock solution is determined by multiplying the above number by the dilution rate of the fertilizer proportioner.

TABLE 6–5
Liquid Fertilization: Calculating Dosage

When liquid fertilization is used on a periodic basis, the dosage of fertilizer may be calculated as follows:

- **Step 1:** Determine dosage based on light intensity and plant category suggested in Figure 6–1 and determine the fertilizer analysis from the label on the fertilizer container. The three numbers, such as 20–20–20, state the analysis for nitrogen, phosphoric acid, and potash. We will use the first number, that for nitrogen.

- **Step 2:** Divide 100 by the first number in the analysis. This gives the weight of the fertilizer to yield 1 gram of nitrogen.

- **Step 3:** Multiply the answer from step 2 by the dosage determined from Figure 6–1. This gives the yearly dosage for this fertilizer.

- **Step 4:** Divide answer from step 3 by number of applications to be made per year. This gives the dosage application.

- **Step 5:** Dissolve the fertilizer weight determined in step 4 in 1 quart of water.

- **Step 6:** Normal irrigation with the fertilizer solution from step 5. Calculation for container size is not necessary because the amount of water held by the soil in the different containers will give the different dosages for containers automatically. Irrigation should be to normal wetting and leaching of the soil.

TABLE 6–6
Dry Fertilization: Calculating Dosage

When dry fertilization is used, the per application dosage of fertilizer may be calculated as follows:

Step 1: Determine dosage based on light intensity and plant category suggested in Figure 6–1 and determine analysis of fertilizer to be used from the label on the fertilizer container. The three numbers tell the analysis for nitrogen, phosphoric acid, and potash. We are interested in using the first number.

Step 2: Divide 100 by the first number in the analysis. This gives the weight of fertilizer to yield 1 gram of nitrogen.

Step 3: Multiply the answer from step 2 by the dosage determined from Figure 6–1 on the basis of the light intensity and the type of plant. This gives the yearly dosage for this fertilizer.

Step 4: Multiply the answer from step 3 by the container size (diameter) factor:

Container Diameter	Factor
3	0.31
4	0.56
5	0.71
6	1.00
8	1.68
10	2.50
12	3.85
14	5.00

This gives the yearly dosage for the container size.

Step 5: Divide the answer from step 4 by the number of applications per year. This gives the dosage per application for the container size.

Step 6: To obtain the approximate volume of fertilizer to apply, use a factor that 1 level teaspoon of fertilizer contains approximately 5 grams of fertilizer. Thus, dividing the answer to step 5 by 5 gives the teaspoonfuls of fertilizer to apply at each application.

SALINITY

Salinity will be a major problem. It can increase because the plant is not growing rapidly and therefore taking up added nutrients. Salinity can increase because of the salts in the irrigation water.

Added injury can occur due to infrequent irrigation, that is, irrigation only after the soil dries out. Salts in the soil become concentrated. For example, if you place a teaspoon of salt in a quart of water, the resulting

TABLE 6–7
Types of Controlled-release Fertilizers for Interior Landscapes

Controlled-release fertilizers may be applied as a surface topping or may be inserted into the soil in various places. It is not necessary for the fertilizer to be mixed throughout the soil to be effective. The dosage should be based on Figure 6–1 and consider the plant requirements and the light intensity.

CATEGORY	SPECIFIC TYPES	COMMENTS
Slowly soluble	MagAmp	Contains ammonium form of nitrogen and high amounts of phosphorus. Rate of release depends on particle size.
	IBDU	Hydrolysis is first step in release. Rate of release depends on particle size, temperature, as well as other factors.
Bacterial decomposition	Urea-formaldehyde	Release rate depends on particle size and temperature. Usually lasts for approximately 3 months under normal interior conditions.
Exchange resin		Nutrient elements adhere to resin and are removed by the plant.
Coated	Osmocote®	Thickness of coating, together with temperature, regulates availability. Various formulations are available giving up to 14 months of release.
	Sulfur coated	Bacterial decomposition of coating also a factor in regulating release.

solution is not very salty, and your taste will tell you it is not. Allow one-half of the water to evaporate or be removed by absorption by plant roots, and the salt is twice as concentrated. Each time more water evaporates, the salt becomes more concentrated. Eventually, it is too salty for you. It is too salty for the plants as well. The plant will absorb excess amounts, leading to leaf burn, or the roots will be injured.

To control salinity problems, avoid applying fertilizers and poor quality water that would add salts to the soil mixture. Flush away any excess salts with water. Reduce the amount of fertilizer you apply and apply good-quality water. It may be necessary to use deionized water at times and in certain places.

Not allowing the soil to become dry, and therefore keeping the salts diluted, may be difficult to achieve. Achieving this depends upon the frequency with which you apply water. At best, this could be a chancey solution, particularly if you are attempting to keep the plants on a dry regime.

Flushing away or leaching excess salts is often difficult to achieve with interior plantings. Where will the excess water go? Furthermore, it is difficult to leach or flush away salts from soils in containers. Flushing can be accomplished if the containers are in planters that have excellent drainage connected with adequate-sized pipes to a sewer system or subsoil that allows water to drain away rapidly. To flush, five times the normal amount of water should be applied and allowed to drain through the soil in the container. Some 15 to 30 minutes after the excess water has stopped draining, an equal amount of water is applied. To be most effective, the entire top of the soil should be flooded. True, sprinkling the water over the entire soil surface would be more effective, but this would be difficult to do in interior plantings.

WATER

The factor that is most difficult to learn to manage properly is irrigation or water management—when and how to apply water. It is difficult to learn to do this properly because most people taking care of plants want to use either a simple formula or a time schedule. Proper water management depends on integrating many considerations, such as the type of plant used, the size of the plant in relation to the volume of soil in which the roots are growing, the soil moisture, and the indoor environment.

Approaching water management properly, one must accept some truisms. The plant is less likely to suffer adverse effects if one fails to water for a day or so than if it is kept constantly moist. The plant will tell you how frequently it must be watered.

Most plants will withstand and look well with dryer soils than is commonly recommended. True, the plant will not be growing as rapidly, but then plant growth indoors is not entirely satisfactory. Drying out the plant, that is, keeping it on an infrequent irrigation regime, will produce more desirable new growth. Even if most plants wilt, they will not die unless the condition persists too long. So the fact is that plants should be allowed to dry out before water is applied. A word of caution: wilting is not an indication of dry soil in all cases. Waterlogged soil, diseased roots, or injured roots can lead to wilting. Always check the soil to determine water content before adding water.

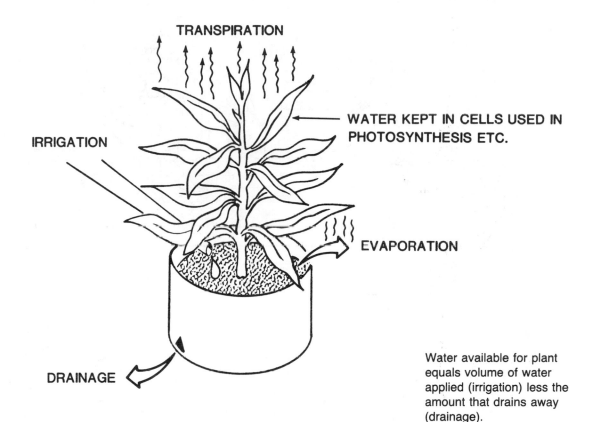

ET or evapotranspiration equals transpiration plus evaporation.

TRANSPIRATION

WATER KEPT IN CELLS USED IN PHOTOSYNTHESIS ETC.

IRRIGATION

EVAPORATION

Water available for plant equals volume of water applied (irrigation) less the amount that drains away (drainage).

DRAINAGE

WHAT HAPPENS TO WATER AP-
PLIED TO SOIL IN CONTAINER
WITH FOLIAGE PLANT GROWING:
• excess over soil holding capacity
  drains away.
• of the water retained by the soil:
  —a portion used for plant growth
  —a portion used to keep plant
    turgid
  —a portion is transpired
  —a portion evaporates from the
    soil, container wall, etc.
  —a portion remains in the soil

FIGURE 6–2

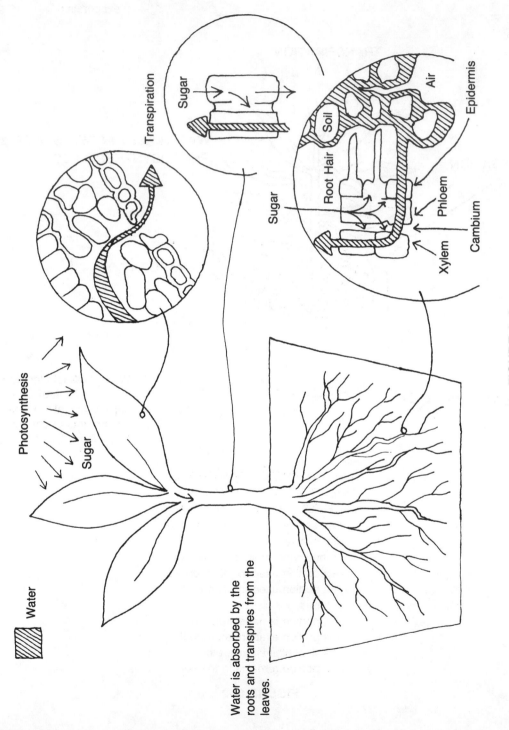

FIGURE 6–3
Water enters plant through roots.

Transpiration

Sugar

Sugar

Air

Soil

Root Hair

Epidermis

Phloem

Cambium

Xylem

Photosynthesis

Sugar

Water

Water is absorbed by the roots and transpires from the leaves.

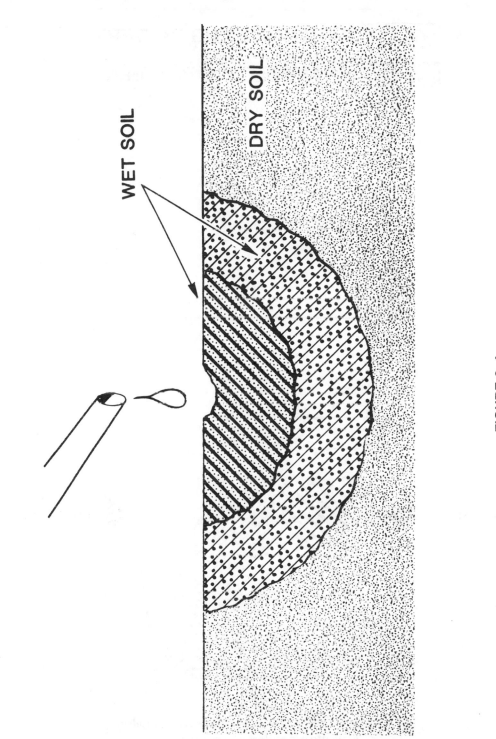

FIGURE 6–4
Usual wetting pattern of uniform texture soil outdoors. Shape of wet zone depends on soil.

WET SOIL

DRY SOIL

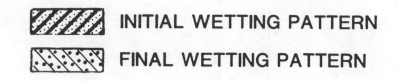

INITIAL WETTING PATTERN

FINAL WETTING PATTERN

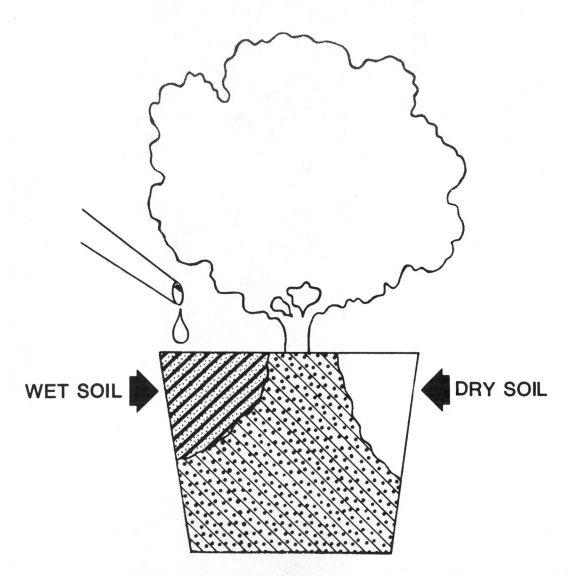

WET SOIL → ← DRY SOIL

FIGURE 6–5
Average container soil mix—wet soil following
irrigation applied at one spot.

When to Irrigate?   By checking the soil, you can tell by feel whether the soil is moist or dry. Feeling the soil is the best indication. Experienced horticulturists can tell when water is needed by several ways, such as rapping the side of a clay pot with a metal object and listening to the tone, by the appearance of the plant, and by determining the weight of the soil, container, and plant.

One may determine when to irrigate by considering that the soil is a bank from which water is removed and to which you add water. If you know how much water is withdrawn and how much water is held in the soil that contains the roots, then you can keep a daily log to determine when to irrigate. For example, it was determined that small plants of *Aglaonema commutatum elegans* used approximately 16 milliliters of water per day in a test situation, and that under the same conditions small plants of *Maranta leuconeura* used approximately 25 milliliters. If both plants were growing in a soil that held 500 milliliters of water that would be available to the plants, then the *Aglaonema* should go 31 days before irrigation is needed, and the *Maranta* should go 20 days.

One must be careful of frequent irrigations. Keeping the soil constantly wet could result in the roots starving for oxygen. Also, under these conditions the possibility of root diseases is increased. It is very important that irrigation be more closely managed in soils with low porosity than where the soil is more porous.

All meters and devices that claim to tell whether the soil is wet or not are not entirely accurate and must be used only as a guide to the water status of the soil. Meter readings must be considered in relation to what the plant tells you.

Tensiometers are the most accurate method of determining the moisture status of the soil. However, these must be regularly serviced to ensure that they consistently give accurate readings. All the probes that use an electric current are not entirely reliable. In addition to the moisture content of the soil, the amount of soluble salts in the soil will influence the reading. Also, constant probing of the soil can injure roots.

How Much Water to Apply?   When the soil reaches the proper dryness for water to be applied, you should apply enough to completely wet all the soil; then add some more to leach out the excess soluble salts. The amount of excess water to apply depends upon the salinity or salt content of the water used to irrigate. If distilled or rain water is used, very little excess need be applied. However, if the water contains salts of 600 to 1000 parts per million, an additional one-fourth or more of the water applied must be allowed to leach away from the root zone; otherwise, the amount of salts in the soil continues to increase.

The amount of water to apply then is a function of the water-holding capacity of the soil and the amount of salts contained in the water. The water-holding capacity of the soil can be determined. Water quality tests can be made to determine the salt content of the irrigation water. Both of these pieces of information should be available to the maintenance person.

How Should Water Be Applied?   Generally, manual procedures should be used, carrying water from planter to planter. The use of automatic irrigation systems is to be discouraged for interior plantings. For large planters, irrigation systems may be installed to distribute the water to the soil. Here tube or drip systems should be installed, and sprinklers are to be generally avoided. However, these systems should be controlled manually. The use of automatic systems will only lead to problems in most cases.

Carrying water to many small planters can be quite a chore. Tank cars can be developed that will allow the easy carrying of fairly large volumes of water; and by using an air pressure or electric pump, or even a battery-operated pump, water can be placed precisely to the soil of each planter.

Keep pots out of water. Containers with soil mixtures should not remain in water. Excess water should be removed from the saucers or pans under the containers.

PRUNING

Pruning, that is, the selective removal of a portion of the plant, should be practiced for any of the following reasons: (1) controlling the size of the plant to remain effective in the space allotted, (2) removal of dead or injured leaves or shoots, and (3) developing and maintaining the shape of the plant to be effective.

Before undertaking interior plant maintenance where pruning will be required, several facts must be faced and several questions answered. Plants that grow under interior landscape conditions will not be as dense as similar plants grown outdoors. Thus, maintaining a tight ball or some other shape will be difficult. Furthermore, plant growth indoors will be much slower than if the conditions are optimum for plant growth. Thus, severely pruned plants will remain unsightly for extended periods of time.

Two basic questions must be answered. First, would it be better to remove the plant and replace it with another similar plant because the pruning required would be so severe as to destroy the effectiveness for extended periods of time? If most of the leaves are partially dead and must be partially or totally removed, or if the shoots to be removed are so large as to require major pruning, it would be better to remove the plant. The removed plant could be reconditioned for use later in another situation. Second, when during the day would be the best time to prune? Maintenance for plants in shopping malls and the like should be done when the general public is not around. Furthermore, pruning when residents are in the building may lead to unhappiness among the residents, because pruning may be looked upon as destroying the plant.

Tips on pruning equipment and procedures are illustrated in Figures 6–6, 6–7, and 6–8.

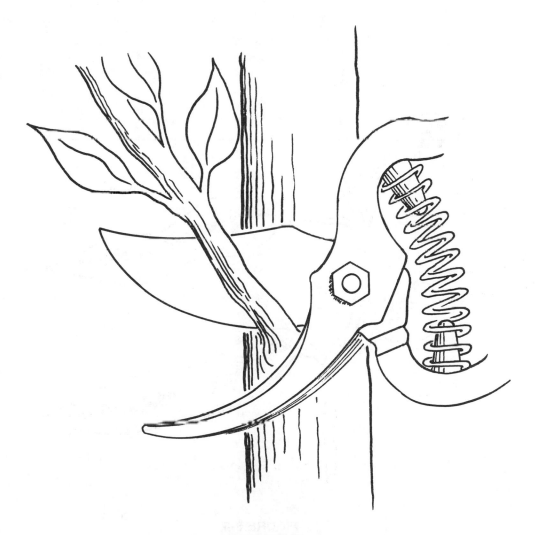

FIGURE 6–6
Correct use of pruner to cut close to branch.

As a matter of policy, the following is suggested. Frequent light prunings, that is, removal of the shoots or shoot tips when they are small and young, could result in better appearing plants than infrequent severe prunings. Second, when a portion of the leaf is dead and must be removed for appearance's sake, removal of the entire leaf is preferred to cutting away the injured portion. Third, when shoots are removed, the cut must be made close to the originating stem.

FIGURE 6–7
When a portion of the leaf is dead or injured,
remove the entire leaf.

FIGURE 6–8
To maintain shape, remove the growing shoot
tips at frequent intervals.

PESTS

For the best results and for the best public relations, pest control should be a mixture of inspection, preventing the introduction of pests, and, where insects or other pests are found, early detection and nonchemical methods of control. Only as a last resort should chemical means of control be used.

All plants should be minutely inspected before installation into an interior landscape to assure freedom from pests—insects, weeds, and diseases. If a suspicion of the existence of pests is raised, the plants should be isolated and proper curative measures taken.

All plants should be examined weekly for pests. Aphids, mites, mealybugs, and scales are the most common pests. Whitefly and fungus gnats

FIGURE 6–9
To maintain or change shape, remove shoots,
making the cut close to the older stems.

are also troublesome. Weekly inspection will ensure early detection of the pests and allow for corrective action before the infection becomes widespread or unsightly.

Nonchemical methods of control of pests include cutting away the infected portion of the plant, provided it does not destroy the appearance, and washing the leaves and stems; soapy water may be used provided the plant is rinsed with clear water afterward. If the entire plant is severely infested, remove and substitute.

As a rule, plants in the interior of buildings should not be treated with pesticides. Pesticides are toxic, and if they are allowed to persist or are

TABLE 6–8
Common Pests of Foliage Plants and Suggested Nonchemical Control

Aphids	Soft-bodied, long-legged insects, usually found on tender growing shoots. Cut away affected portion, wash plant with water; soapy water can be used provided the plant is rinsed immediately afterward.
Mealybugs	Usually seen as white cottony mass on plant, often in leaf axils. If infection is small, swab insects with rubbing alcohol.
Scales	Many types; usually appear as a brown, raised object attached to the leaf or stem. Remove affected parts. In severe cases, remove plant. Coating the scale with oil will help to control insect.
Mites	Small "spiders" that feed mainly on undersides of leaves. Barely visible to the naked eye. First symptoms noticed may be leaf with gray to gray-green spots. Wash plant. Remove severely infected plant (plants with webs on them or with web hanging down from the leaves).
Whiteflys	Small, white flies that feed on the leaves.
Fungus gnats	Dark gnats, the larva of which feeds on the organic matter in the soil and on soft stem or root tissue. Larva white in color with a dark head.

taken into the air-movement system of the building they could cause problems. Remember that people smell and touch plants. Unless a pesticide is registered for such use, one cannot legally use the pesticide in that situation. Furthermore, public relations would be better served if pesticides were not used in buildings. Thus, if plants are infected to the point where nonchemical controls are not effective, they should be removed. These may be taken back to the nursery for rehabilitation, or if the problem is too severe, they should be destroyed.

Table 6–8 lists some common pests and nonchemical controls for them.

PLANT DISEASES

Unfortunately, the plants used indoors for interior landscaping are susceptible to many diseases, from leaf spotting to stem cankers to rotting of the stems and roots. Under interior conditions, it is often impossible to cure a disease; the only practical solution is to remove and replace the plant.

Leaf spots are very common; they are caused by fungus and bacterial sources. Different environmental conditions favor different diseases; warm and wet conditions favor *Alternaria*, *Erwinia*, and *Cylindrocladium* organisms, while warm days and cool nights favor the gray mold botrytis. Thus, changing the environment for the control of one disease may lead to another. Removal of infected leaves may be a method of controlling these diseases indoors.

Rotting of the plant tissue usually calls for the removal of the plant. Under certain circumstances where the rotting is on a branch or leaf, cutting away the affected portion with sterile instruments may be a method of eliminating the disease.

Rotting of the roots is very common. Usually the first sign noted is wilting of the plant and failure to recover when water is applied. Plants infected with root rots should be replaced.

Likewise, plants infected with viral diseases should be replaced. Viral diseases usually appear as distorted plants or as unusual changes in color.

Little can be said to recommend the use of fungicides indoors for the control of diseases. Many chemicals are not registered for such use. Furthermore, protecting people during application and from residues presents many serious problems.

What Is the Cure?   Despite the best intentions and seemingly the best care the plant can receive, from time to time one or more plants will show obvious distress. This can happen to the best of maintenance companies and often may be due to things others have done to the plants unbeknownst to the service personnel.

Whenever anything goes wrong, the problem must be corrected. Often the solution is to replace plants with new and healthy ones. However, that is not always possible. Then detective work is necessary to pinpoint the cause and to effect a cure. The simple tasks, such as the identification of an insect, are usually easily accomplished. More difficult symptoms are those growth distortions, discolorations, or leaf fall that may be caused by any of a number of possibilities. Do not overlook the obvious solution. At the same time, do not be misled with the obvious answer. For example, overwatering causes many of the problems associated with interior landscapes. While the cause of the problem may be overwatering, the reasons the plants are overwatered is not always so obvious. Are the maintenance people doing a poor job? Or is someone watering the plants between visits of the maintenance people because he or she wants to care for the plants? Or is someone pouring excess coffee onto the soil instead of disposing of the coffee in the proper place?

GUIDES TO PLANT PROBLEMS

The checklist of things to consider or questions to ask given in Table 6–9 should be helpful as a guide to ensure that all important questions are asked and to narrow down the possibilities to a manageable few. In addition, the catalog of symptoms and possible causes given in Table 6–10 will be helpful.

TABLE 6–9
Checklist of Questions to Help Pinpoint Cause of
Abnormal Plant Growth

	QUESTIONS TO ASK
The Environment	• Hot air draft from heater striking plants?
	• Cold air draft from air-conditioner vent or from opening door?
	• Enough light or too much light at certain times of day?
	• Location near coffee room, cafeteria, or other areas where coffee, soft drinks or other liquids may be poured onto the soil?
	• People sitting on planter and crushing plant or compacting soil?
	• Paint fumes; was the area recently painted?
	• Cleaning solvents fumes caused injury?
	• Toxic fumes from any source?
The Planter	• Excess water drains away?
	• Planter sides or bottom or both coated with toxic compound?
	• Drains clear and open?
	• Are containers plunged into the soil or are the plants planted in the soil?
The Soil	• Is the soil heavy or light?
	• Is the management of irrigation and fertilization suited for the soil?
	• Have different soil mixes been placed in the same planter? If so, are they being irrigated at different intervals?

(continued on following page)

TABLE 6–9 (Continued)

QUESTIONS TO ASK	
Cultural Practices	• Is the soil allowed to dry sufficiently between irrigations?
	• What is the quality of the irrigation water?
	• How much water is applied at each irrigation?
	• How much fertilizer is used and how frequently are the plants fertilized?
	• How frequently have the plants been pruned?
	• Were the plants established in a container before they were placed in the interior planting?
The Plant	• What does the abnormal growth pattern look like?
	• Is the abnormality general or localized?

TABLE 6–10
Frequently Observed Symptoms and Possible Causes

SYMPTOM	POSSIBLE CAUSES
A. Object attached to or on plant	
1. Object can be brushed off	• Empty skin of insects
	• Deposit from hard water
	• Deposit from fertilizer spray
	• Residue from pesticides
	• Dust, soot, etc.
	• Fecal matter from insects
	• Dead insects
	• Weed seeds
2. Firmly attached	
a. White, cottony mass on stems or on roots	• Mealybug
b. Small, white waxy mass	• Scale
c. Small, whitish or translucent objects, may be on a stalk	• Insect eggs

TABLE 6–10 (Continued)

SYMPTOM	POSSIBLE CAUSES
d. Small, hard, round, or elongated spots	• Scale
	• Edema, a physiological disorder
	• Disease on some plants
e. Whitish powder	• Powdery mildew
f. Brownish or reddish film	• High iron in water leaving deposit
	• Heavy false spider mite infestation
g. Fine web on leaf or between leaves	• Spider mite infestation
	• Mite infestation
h. Greenish deposit	• Algae
i. Blackish deposit	• Sooty mold growth or honeydew from insects
3. Moves about freely	• Mites
	• Thrips
	• Aphids
4. Fly from plant when disturbed	• Whitefly
	• Fungus gnats
B. Plant color changed	
1. Lighter green than normal	
a. Uniform throughout	• Nitrogen deficiency
	• Excessively bright lights
	• High temperatures
b. Speckled	• Spider mite infestation
2. Purple color of older leaves	• Phosphorus deficiency
	• Cold temperature
3. Yellowing	
a. In young leaves	• Deficiency of iron, manganese, copper, or zinc
	• Excess of manganese
	• Phytotoxicity from chemicals
	• Overwatering
	• Root nematode infestation

(continued on the following pages)

TABLE 6–10 (Continued)

SYMPTOM	POSSIBLE CAUSES
b. In older leaves	• Deficiency of potassium, magnesium
	• Excess soil salinity
	• Overwatering
	• Cold drafts
	• Too low light intensity
	• Soil mix poorly aerated
	• Excessive drying of soil
	• Chemical phytotoxicity
	• Air pollution, sulfur dioxide
	• Insect feeding, thrips, leafhoppers
4. Yellow spots	
a. Regular, round spots	• Fungal infection
	• Bacterial infection
	• Injury from application of pesticide or fertilizer
	• Air pollution injury
b. Irregular or odd shapes	• Cold water injury
	• Fungal or bacterial infection
	• Viral infection
	• Injury from pesticide or fertilizer application
	• Air pollution injury
5. Water-soaked or greasy appearing spots	• Early stage of high temperature injury
	• Early stage of cold temperature injury
	• Bacterial or fungal disease
	• Foliar nematode infection
6. New color pattern	• Viral infection
	• Genetic change
7. Normal variegated color becoming green	• Excess fertilizer
	• Low light intensity
	• Genetic change
	• Too short daily dark period

TABLE 6–10 (Continued)

SYMPTOM	POSSIBLE CAUSES
C. Plant growth disturbed	
1. Plant tops not growing	• Mite infestation
	• Nutrient deficiency: copper, boron, calcium, zinc
	• Insufficient lights
2. Older leaves misshaped	• Air pollution
	• Virus infection
	• Phytotoxicity from chemical
3. Newer leaves misshaped	• Nutrient deficiency: copper, zinc, boron, calcium
	• Mite infestation
	• Insect infestation
	• Plant hormone used
	• Phytotoxicity from pesticides
4. Stems thin and elongated	• Low light intensity
	• Excess fertilizer
	• Excessively high temperatures
5. Petioles thin and elongated	• Low light intensity
6. Abnormal holes in leaf	• Insect, slug, or snail infestation
	• Mechanical injury
7. Leaves or flowers falling from plant	• Plants not properly conditioned
	• Improper water application; lack of water or overwatering
	• Chilling injury
	• Roots cut when transplanted
	• Roots cut when cultivating or maintaining plants
	• Air pollution, especially ethylene, also ammonia
	• High soil salinity
	• Mite infestation associated with lack of water or drying air currents
	• Chemical injury

(continued on the following pages)

125

TABLE 6–10 (Continued)

SYMPTOM	POSSIBLE CAUSES
8. Fasciated growth	• Genetic change • Viral infection • Disease infection
9. Gall growth	• Disease infection; crown gall (some plants have normal tuberous growth that appear similar to crown gall) • Nematodes (on roots)
10. New leaves do not develop normal split or normal holes	• Too low light intensity • Vine no longer clinging to support and climbing
11. Few lateral branches	• Too low light intensity
12. Leaves wilting	• High soil salinity • Insufficient soil water • Cold soils • High air temperatures • Low air humidity • Root rot diseases • Root nematodes • Root mealybugs
D. Plant tissue killed	
1. Small spots	• Air pollution • Disease infection
2. Irregular spots	• Cold water injury • Leaf miner feeding • Disease infection • Foliar nematode infestation • Sun scorch • Cold temperatures • Air pollution • Chemical injury: pesticides, fertilizer
3. Leaf tip dead	• Excess soil salinity • Low temperature injury • High temperature injury

TABLE 6–10 (Continued)

SYMPTOM	POSSIBLE CAUSES
4. Leaf margin dead	• Deficiency of potassium
	• Excess boron, fluorine
	• High temperature injury
	• Low temperature injury
	• Lack of water
5. Stem killed	
a. At soil line	• Disease
	• High soil salinity
	• Dry fertilizer against stem
	• Overwatering
	• Poorly drained soil
	• Fungus gnat infestation
	• Phytotoxicity from pesticides
b. On stem above soil line	• Disease
	• Sun scorch
	• Mechanical injury
c. Twig dies back	• Nutrient deficiency: boron, calcium, copper
	• Plant desiccated
	• Fungus disease
	• Phytotoxicity from pesticides
6. Roots dead	• Root rot diseases
	• Soil too wet

CHAPTER SEVEN
Plants for the Interior Landscape

The number of different plants that can be used in interior landscapes is endless. Often the secret is to learn how to manage the plant rather than whether the plant is adaptable to the interior situation. For example, it is often stated that Japanese maple will not make a satisfactory interior plant. True, if a plant is in full leaf when moved indoors, the leaves will fall and the plant will fail to grow because the leaves are not adapted to low light intensity, and growth will not occur because of the dormancy of the buds. However, if a plant is moved indoors just before spring growth occurs, the leaves that develop will be adapted to the indoor conditions and will remain on the plant. The plant will remain attractive for several weeks to months, depending on the care it receives.

Every year, many more plants are introduced for use in interior conditions. These plants come from plant explorers that find adaptable plants and bring them into cultivation. Other plants are developed by hybridizers. Whatever the source, we are fortunate to receive the bounty.

Some plants are more adaptable than others. In each interior location, adapted plants should be used.

Much can be said about plants in addition to their adaptability. Part of the satisfaction each person receives from interior plantings will be from their knowledge about the individual plants. We can help to weave a spell around the plants. Fortunately, there is a lot of legend, a lot of usefulness besides decoration, and a lot of mysticism associated with the plants we use indoors. Some of this information is discussed with the individual plants.

This section is not intended to be a comprehensive treatment of the more adapted plants. Rather, the intent is to discuss some of the more useful, more adapted plants, and to mention some little used plants that could be very useful.

This section is intended to be the starting place for those involved with interior plantings. One should build on this group of plants, revise, and delete for each location and for each business.

ACANTHUS FAMILY (ACANTHACEAE)

Some of the plants in the acanthus family are spiny; thus the name for the genus *Acanthus* was derived from the Greek name for a spine. Several are used indoors. Most of the plants are broadleaved evergreens with colorful or shapely leaves. In the tropics, many are used for medicinal purposes. Some have served as food, and at least one has been used to repel insects from clothing.

The zebra plant, *Aphelandra squarrosa*, has colorful inflorescences. Colorful bracts enclose small but often colorful flowers. Other characteristics of value are the colorful leaves in pairs on each side of a square stem. *Aphelandra squarrosa* 'Dania' was discovered in Denmark. Leaves are deep green with white or creamy veins. Stems are reddish-brown. Inflorescence has orange-yellow bracts and yellow flowers. Indoors, plants, which may become quite large, should be kept in moderate to high light conditions.

The nerve plant, *Fittonia verchaffeltii* var. *argyroneura* is a spreading, tropical herbaceous plant. Oval-shaped leaves are in pairs colored vivid green with many white veins. Moderate to high light conditions and moist soils are needed.

Hemigraphis has silver to purple green leaves on the top and a reddish to purplish underside of the leaf. In the tropics it is used in large beds as a groundcover that requires very little care. Several types are available for interior use.

Hemigraphis alternata (Hemigraphis colorate), a native of Java, has a silvery violet upperside of the leaf and is red-purple beneath. The common name of red ivy is given to this plant.

A variety known as *H. exotica*, the purple waffle plant, has puckered leaves that are metallic purplish-green on the top and wine-red beneath. A narrow leaf form, *H. repanda*, is native to Malaysia. In Malaysia, *Hemigraphis* is used medicinally. The plants will do well in low light and should be kept moderately moist.

AROIDS OR THE ARUM FAMILY (ARACEAE)

From the viewpoint of the number of individual species and cultivars that do well indoors, none exceeds the aroids, or the arum family. Characteristic of the family is the Jack-in-the-pulpit inflorescence. Flowers are actually small and without petals; they are contained on a stalk known as a spadix. Surrounding the spadix, or in some cases opening flat as a colorful leaf, is the spathe. All genera that have colorful flowers such as the *Anthurium* and *Spathiphyllum* have a colorful spathe.

The sap of many aroids contains oxalic acid that leads to the formation of calcium oxalate crystals. These are irritants rather than poisons. Calcium oxalate crystals enter the skin and cause swelling and inflammation. Treating the area with a weak acid such as vinegar (acetic acid) dissolves the crystals.

Ornamentation is not the only use of the aroids. Fruit of *Monstera deliciosa* is eaten much like corn on the cob, but the oxalate crystals must be washed off. Taro, a staple in the South Pacific, is made from the starchy rootstock of another aroid. Calcium oxalate within the plant is dissipated by crushing and heating. The tender shoots of another aroid are called Carribe cabbage. Some aroids are used as medicine.

From Japan, the miniature sweet flag *Acorus gramineus* cv. *variegatus* is 4 to 12 inches high. It looks like a dwarfed iris or grass. Leaves are light green with white variegations. This plant needs plenty of water and is best at medium light in warm locations.

The Chinese evergreens *(Aglaonema)* are, as the name implies, natives of China; they are slow-growing, small plants that remain attractive and withstand a lot of abuse, poor conditions, and neglect. They may be grown with the roots in water only. The stems are fleshy, holding the plants upright when small, but with age the stems recline under the weight of the crown. An exudation from the leaves may spot wood finishes.

The silver evergreen, *Aglaonema commutatum* var. *maculatum* (often sold as *A. commutatum*), has deep green leaves marked with silver gray, showy white flowers and red- to yellow-colored fruit. Indoors, the best conditions are a warm location, low to medium light intensity, and moist to dry soil.

Golden evergreen, *Aglaonema commutatum* 'White Rajah,' has leaves with markings of light green, silver, and yellow. Often you will find this plant called A. *pseudobracteatum*. A warm location, low to medium light intensity, and moist to dry soil suits this plant.

The plant most commonly known as the Chinese evergreen is *Aglaonema modestum*. For a long time, and even today in many places, Chinese evergreens are sold as A. *simplex*. The differences between these two species are difficult to see, thus the confusion. Both have solid green leaves. *Aglaonema modestum* leaves are wider and flatter. The Chinese evergreen should be kept warm, in medium light with moist to dry soil.

How often we see anthurium flowers along with orchid leis as passengers deplane from Hawaii, the center of commercial anthuriums for floral arrangements. The cut flowers last for weeks. Native of the tropical Americas, anthuriums as a whole require a rather coarse soil (mostly grown in cinders, bark, or between logs) composed mainly of organic materials, a warm, humid atmosphere, and partial shade. Among the many species is the flamingo flower, A. *scherzerianum*, the pigtail anthurium. Also called the flame plant, the flowers are red to salmon, with a golden-yellow twisted and coiled spadix. While a few flowers are present throughout the year, the largest number occurs from February to July. Indoors give the plant high light intensity but not direct sunlight, and maintain a moist soil at all times.

Dieffenbachia, or dumbcane, are natives of the American tropics; they are plants with bold texture, colorful leaves, and giant size. They contain calcium oxalate, which can cause inflammation and swelling of the mouth and tongue, as well as affect the vocal cords—thus the common name. Calcium oxalate is not a poison, however, and its painful effects will eventually subside. Dumbcanes are very tolerant plants that do well in all indoor conditions. Most suitable are medium light intensity and moist to dry soils.

Many cultivars have been introduced over the years. Among the more useful species and cultivars are the following:

- *D. amoena*, giant dumbcane, mother-in-law plant or tuftroot with large 12- to 18-inch leaves that have white blotches.

- *D.* 'Exotica,' a cultivar of unknown parentage; the smallish leaves, 8 to 10 inches long, have cream white variegations.

- *D. picta*, 'Rudolph Roehrs'; one of the many cultivars of *D. picta*, this has an almost completely yellow to chartreuse leaf with blotches of white and a green midrib and leaf edge or margin.

- *D. picta* 'Superba' is another variant of the species with thicker leaves and more creamy white variegations.

Often called the Swiss-cheese plants, plants in the genus *Monstera* have entire, somewhat heart-shaped juvenile leaves. As the plant climbs and matures, the leaves become larger, perforated, and divided. The most common species is *Monstera deliciosa*, the ceriman or Mexican breadfruit. The fruit is edible. The juvenile form is commonly sold as *Philodendron pertusum*. Where sufficient elbow room exists, this plant should be given medium light intensity and moist soils.

Philodendrons may possibly be the most important single genus from the viewpoint of the number and adaptability of plants used indoors. Two plant forms are found in this genus, vines that climb rapidly and self-heading plants that become arborescent with age, forming a trunk with a crown of leaves. The self-heading species are more tolerant of cold than the vining species. In both groups, the juvenile foliage is remarkably different from the mature form; the form most commonly seen is juvenile.

Many cultivars and hybrids have been developed. Among the most useful indoor plants are *P. domesticum*, often called *P. hastatum*, with leaves to 1 foot long and performing best where the light is medium and the soil is moist. *Philodendron* x 'Emerald Queen' is a hybrid that is quite resistant to disease, cold tolerant, and has exceptional keeping qualities; it tolerates low light conditions well, but is best at medium light with moist soils. *Philodendron scandens* subsp. *oxycardium*, the heart-leaf philodendron, was sold for years as *P. cordatum*, and it still is. Like the other philodendrons, this species does best at medium light, but does well in low light if growth is not encouraged. The soil should be kept dry. The unusual horse's head or fiddle-shaped leaf of *P. panduriforme* gives this climbing philodendron its common name. Of the self-heading group, *P. selloum* and *P.* x *Wend-imbe* are excellent choices. *Philodendron selloum* is very cold tolerant and forms large, divided leaves to 3 feet across with age. The underside of the leaf of the hybrid *P.* x *Wend-imbe* is pink. All philodendrons do their best indoors in medium light with the soil kept moist to dry. They are very tolerant of low light conditions, where the soil should be kept dry.

Another aroid vine, *Epipremnum* (often called pothos) is an excellent indoor plant, having heart-shaped juvenile leaves of various colors. The juvenile leaf form is most commonly seen. *Epipremnum aureum* (formerly *Scindapsus aureus*), the devil's ivy, has small green and yellow heart-shaped juvenile foliage and large, divided and perforated, green and yellow mature foliage. To maintain the adult foliage, the plant must remain attached to and continue climbing a support such as a tree. Dry soils and medium light conditions should lead to long, attractive life.

White anthuriumlike flowers are an attraction of the genus *Spathiphyllum*. These plants form a clump of leaves, unlike the anthurium, which tends to climb. The plants will tolerate low light conditions but need medium light intensities to flower. The soil should be moist. White flag, *S. clevelandii,* has large 4- to 6-inch flowers that become green with age. The white anthurium, *S.* x 'Mauna Loa' is a hybrid of compact habit and is very floriferous. The pure white flowers may be 8 inches long on very old plants.

Syngonium species and cultivars have arrow-shaped juvenile leaves that become lobed and palmately (like fingers on your hand) divided when mature. Indoors, medium light conditions and moist soils are best. These plants can be grown with the roots in only water. *Syngonium podophyllum,* for indoor use, was sold as *Nephthytis afzeli* and *N. liberica.* Many cultivars are available; two useful ones are the following:

- *S. augustatum* 'Albolineatum': the center of the heart-shaped or three-lobed leaf is silver-white. May be found as *Nephthytis triphyllum.*
- *S. podophyllum* 'Trileaf Wonder.' The mature segmented leaf forms very early on this cultivar.

ARALIAS (ARALIACEAE)

A rather diverse group of trees, shrubs, and herbs make up this family. Uses made of these plants have been environmental, medicinal, and for paper. Many plants are used in outdoor landscaping; these same plants find a happy home indoors. English ivy, *Hedera helix,* is an example. Paper was made from the rice paper plant, *Tetrapanax papyriferum,* and parts of many plants have been used medicinally. In the Orient, for example, the ginseng *Panax pseudoginseng* is supposed to have many beneficial properties and has long been used as an aphrodisiac.

A large tree in its native Queensland, Australia, the schefflera, *Brassaia actinophylla,* does well in containers, although in dark locations it sheds lower leaves. The plant is often sold under the name *Schefflera actinophylla.* This plant should be given medium to high light and the soil should be kept dry.

Appearing very similar to Schefflera, but more tolerant of indoor conditions, holding the older leaves much better, is the tupidanthus or mallet flower, *Tupidanthus calyptratus.* You can distinguish the two by the number and shape of the leaflets; tupidanthus has more and the leaflets are waxy, plus the fact that tupidanthus branches earlier. Moist soils and medium light conditions should prevail.

The dwarf schefflera is *Schefflera arboricola (Heptapleurum arboricola)*. The cultivar Hawaiian Elf is more attractive than the species. Freely branching, the plant may be shaped into many shapes. It is quite tolerant of adverse conditions.

Aralia is a name applied to many plants, leading to a great deal of confusion. The spider aralia or threadleaf aralia is *Dizygotheca elegantissima*, originally called *Aralia elegantissima*. The graceful, threadlike, reddish juvenile foliage (with age the leaves become broader, coarser, and lobed) and cream-color mottled stem make this a highly attractive indoor plant. This plant should be kept in medium light with moist soil.

Plants in the genus *Polyscias* are also called aralias. These freebranching shrubs have compound leaves of many colors, shapes, and textures. Adaptable to indoor conditions, the plants should be given medium to high light intensities and moist soils. The variegated Balfour aralia, *Polyscias balfouriana marginata*, have roundish leaflets with whitish borders.

The leaves of *Fatsia japonica* are large, up to 15 inches wide, and deeply lobed. Becoming rather large and upright, this plant is excellent indoors in medium to high light conditions with moist soils. It will do well in poor light and cool locations. Several cultivars are available.

A hybrid between *Fatsia japonica* 'Moseri' and *Hedera helix* var. *hibernica* is the miracle plant, or fatshedera *(Fatshedera lizei)*. This plant grows upright like the fatsia, but with a five-lobed leaf more like hedera. While it does well in cool locations with moist soil, it should be given high light for best performance.

The English ivy, *Hedera helix*, is the classical ivy of the temperate zone. The vine climbs, holding to walls with aerial rootlets. The foliage most seen, three to five lobes, is juvenile. Mature foliage is entire on stems that grow away from the wall. The mature form, more difficult to propagate, forms shrubby plants. The English ivy should be given high light and moist soils; they may be grown for long time spans with the roots in water.

Many cultivars of the English ivy, differing in color and shape of the leaf, as well as compactness and rapidity of growth, are available:

- 'California Fan,' fan-shaped, lobed leaf with wavy margins.
- 'Fluffy Ruffles,' roundish leaves with many crests and undulations.
- 'Glacier,' small triangular leaf with center of gray green and edges of white with pink border.
- 'Golddust,' a slow-growing cultivar with three-lobed leaf mottled green and yellow.

- 'Needlepoint,' a bushy compact plant with tiny 1- to 1¼-inch leaves with three lobes of which the center lobe is elongated and sharply pointed.
- 'Shamrock,' the stems of which are red and the side lobes of the leaf are cupped upward.
- 'Scutifolia,' sometimes called 'Sweetheart,' the leaves of which are heart-shaped with a reddish petiole.

MONKEY PUZZLE TREES (ARAUCARIACEAE)

These are tropical trees, mostly with narrow leaves and strange branching formation. Leaves are tough and often tipped with a sharp spine. Some trees of this family are valuable as timber. Seeds of some species are edible.

The Norfolk Island pine, *Araucaria heterophylla*, is often used as a tropical Christmas tree. You may find it under the name A. *excelsa* and also as star pine in California. Cuttings of this plant may be rooted; cuttings from the central upright stem form normal-looking, symmetrical trees, while the cuttings from the side branches form trees of irregular shapes and forms. Norfolk Island pines should be placed in high light conditions with moist soil.

MILKWEED FAMILY (ASCLEPIADACEAE)

Most of the species have a milky sap. Some have strangely shaped parts; one, a tropical epiphyte, has pitcher-shaped leaves that catch rain. Some of the species are poisonous; natives have used them to tip arrows to kill fish and animals. Food, medicine, fiber, and dye are some of the uses or products from plants in this family.

A tropical vine, the wax plant, *Hoya carnosa*, is one of the milkweed family that does beautifully indoors at moderate temperatures, medium to high light conditions, and in dry soils. Preferably, the plant should not be disturbed by repotting. Flowers of the wax plant occur on the same shoot each summer, forming a cluster of small, pinkish-white, waxy flowers; consequently faded flowers should not be cut off. The variegated form, *Hoya carnosa* 'Variegata,' has leaves that have cream to white, sometimes tinged with red, markings.

BEGONIAS (BEGONIACEAE)

The family takes its name after the genus *Begonia*, which was named after a French promoter of botany, Michael Begon. While a few species are used medicinally and a few are eaten, the herbs in this family are mostly for human environmental uses.

Several distinct types of begonias are recognized, some with colorful and showy flowers, others with highly colored leaves. For indoor use, the plants with highly colored leaves are best. The leaf is nearly always lopsided. *Begonia* x 'Cleopatra' is a hybrid with maple-shaped, green with chocolate-red leaves, and pink, fragrant flowers. The plant should be given a warm location, medium to high light intensity, and moist soil.

PINEAPPLE FAMILY (BROMELIACEAE)

The name of this family honors a Swedish botanist, Olans Bromel. Almost all the species come from the subtropical and tropical Americas; some are natives of the southern United States. Spanish moss, *Tillandsia usneoides*, is an example. This epiphyte, hanging from trees, vines, and other things overhead, has been used in various ways—stuffing for mattresses, packing, and shading for other plants.

The most famous of the members of this family is *Ananus comosus* the pineapple. Besides the delicious fruit, a fiber may be obtained from the leaves.

Some bromeliads have been used medicinally by natives.

Many bromeliad species are used in interior landscapes. *Aechmea fasciata*, the silver vase, is among the most popular. Like many bromeliads, the silver vase has a colorful inflorescence as well as beautiful leaves. The cup formed by the leaves should be kept full of water, and the soil may then be kept dry. For best color of foliage, the plant should be in a medium to high light location.

SPIDERWORTS (COMMELINACEAE)

Two Dutch botanists of the early eighteenth century, J. and G. Commelin, are honored by this family. The plants are generally herby with knotty stems. The most important use of the plants in this family has been as part of our environment; minor uses have included medicine and food (starch from the rhizomes of some species).

Moses-in-the-cradle, *Rhoeo spathacea*, so named because of the white flowers peeking out between two bracts that form a boat or cradle shape, has a long, 8- to 12-inch leaf that is green above and purple below. Flowers form at the base of the leaf and are cradled against the stem. Sold quite frequently as *Rhoeo discolor*, this plant is tolerant of indoor conditions, performing best in a dry soil at high light intensities.

Many of the creeping plants are confused; they belong to three genera, *Commelina*, *Tradescantia*, and *Zebrina*. All generally root easily and may be grown in water. The wandering Jew, *Tradescantia fluminensis*, has purplish brown leaves about 2 inches long and purplish beneath. Silver wandering Jew, *Zebrina pendula*, has leaves of about the same size but with silver bands on a green to purple leaf with purple underside. Several cultivars with different leaf colors are available. Both *Tradescantia* and *Zebrina* should be given moist to dry soil where the light intensity is medium.

COMPOSITES (COMPOSITAE)

The aggregation of individual flowers into a head, such as a daisy, is the feature of this family, the largest of the plant kingdom. Many uses have been made of the plants, including medicinal uses, food (lettuce, Jerusalem artichoke), extraction of dye, insecticide, and oils (for food, paint, lubrication). Also included are many of the most popular ornamentals for human environments.

Velvet plant, *Gynura aurantiaca* requires moist soils and high light conditions indoors. The leaves are covered with velvety violet to purple hairs. The veins in the leaves are also purple.

DOGWOODS (CORNACEAE)

Some of the handsomest trees and shrubs belong to the dogwood family; they are outstanding for flowering and fruiting effects, shape of plant, and colorful fall color. Although the plants are primarily ornamental, the fruits of *Cornus mas* and *Cornus capitata* are edible.

The golddust plant—*Aucuba japonica* 'Variegata,' is one of the finest plants for indoor use. This cultivar, with green leaves with yellow spots and blotches, is one of many cultivars of the species. Medium light intensities and moist to dry soils should suit this plant.

ORPINE FAMILY (CRASSULACEAE)

The orpines are succulents; the plants have fleshy leaves and thick cuticles on the leaves. Evaporation of water is so effectively inhibited that detached leaves remain fresh and alive for weeks. Plants have had little economic use aside from ornamentals.

Jade plant, *Crassula argentea,* is very tolerant of indoor conditions. Often sold as *C. arborescens,* but differing from the true *C. arborescens,* the plant has thick stems and fleshy oval-shaped leaves that are flat underneath and convex above. It may be pruned to form bonsai plants adaptable to indoor conditions. Masses of small, white, star-shaped flowers cover the plant during the winter. The plant is most attractive at high light conditions and in dry soil. It will tolerate low light conditions.

Other species of Crassula have different colored leaves; some are creeping while others are upright.

CYCADS (CYCADACEAE)

One of the oldest families, cycads are cone-bearing plants with palmlike habits and compound (pinnate or featherlike) leaves. Some are upright, others creep. Cycads have been used for food; the seeds of some *Cycas* and *Zamia* species are edible; a starch, or sago, which is baked into a bread, is harvested from the pith of others.

Cycads are slow-growing plants. The sago palm, *Cycas revoluta,* is excellent indoors, requiring a minimum of care. The best indoor conditions are medium light intensity and moist to dry soils.

SPURGES (EUPHORBIACEAE)

The family was named in honor of Euphorbus, physician to King Juba. A family of great economic importance, some of the products include oils, fats for burning, medicine (castor oil and croton oil, for example), food, and natural rubber. Natives have used some to tip poison arrows.

Crotons are shrubby plants with colorful leaves of many shapes and sizes. Most of the cultivars are hybrids of the species *Codiaeum variegatum* var. *pictum.* Full sunlight is necessary for the highest color intensity. Indoors the light intensity should be as high as possible and moist soil should be maintained.

'Aucubifolium,' the aucuba-leaf or goldspot croton, as small 3- to 4-inch leaves of bright green blotched and spotted with yellow. The plant resembles *Aucuba japonica* 'Variegata.'

'Elaine,' the lanceleaf croton, has shallowly lobed, lance-shaped, bright green leaves with yellow veins containing tinges of red and pink.

GESNERIADS (GESNERIACEAE)

Named after an early Zurich botanist, Conrad Gesner, the Gesneriads are mostly herbaceous plants whose only economic importance is ornamental. Colorful flowers are present on plants in this family.

Royal red bugler, *Aeschynanthus pulcher*, has flowers measuring 2 to 2½ inches long, vermillion red with a yellow throat. These plants are often sold under the name Trichosporum. A warm, humid location, moderate to high light intensity, and moist soil are the best indoor conditions.

Columnea form vines that in nature grow as epiphytes on trees with the vines hanging down. They have colorful flowers.

Episcia, or the flame violet, has colorful foliage as well as colorful flowers. They must be kept warm (over 65°F) and prefer moderate to high light intensities, wet soils, and humid atmospheres. Episcia *cupreata* 'Acajou' is one of the more colorful cultivars with silver veins in a dark mahogany leaf and orange-red flowers.

MINT FAMILY (LABIATAE)

The unique two-lipped flower gives this family its name and a distinguishing characteristic. Others are the tangled stem and the fragrant oils contained in many of these plants. Mint juleps, chewing gum, or iced tea come to mind as one talks about the mint family. Catnip, hoarhound, and garden sage are some of the plants.

Creeping Charlie, *Plectranthus nummularius*, often sold as *P. parviflorus*, has a waxy, metallic green, round leaf, which is gray-green beneath with purple veins. This plant tolerates abuse. Indoor conditions of medium light and moist soil are preferred.

LILY FAMILY (LILIACEAE)

A distinguishing feature of the plants in the lily family is a bulbous or swollen rootstock. Many of the important indoor plants with long sword-shaped leaves are members.

Economically, the lily family contributes medicine, food (onion, leek), soap from the roots of some yucca, fiber from New Zealand flax (*Phormium tenax*) for fabric, and incense.

Asparagus are fernlike plants with woody stems but without true leaves. The green leaf is really a flattened stem. Several species, such as A. *setaceus*, are used for floral arrangements. The young shoots (spears) of A. *officinalis* are our edible asparagus. Asparagus are tolerant of indoor heat and dry soils. The best conditions to maintain are medium light and moist soils.

'Asparagus fern,' A. *setaceus*, has a lacy frond. The stem may become twining. Plume asparagus, A. *densiflorus* 'Myers,' is a compact grower with a tight plumelike stem. Red fruit form where the air is hot and dry. This plant is often sold as A. *meyerii*. Sprengeri fern, A. *densiflorus* cv. 'Sprengeri' has drooping stems and rather coarse foliage. Fragrant white flowers are followed by red berries when the light intensity is high.

Aspidistra has been used for many years and has the name cast-iron plant because of the plant's tolerance to adverse conditions. Leaves arise from a crown and may be up to 2½ feet long. *Aspidistra elatior* has solid green foliage. The cultivar A. *elatior* 'Variegata' has leaves striped with white. Moist soils, medium light intensity, and moderate temperatures are best.

The spider plant, *Chlorophytum comosum* 'Vittatum,' forms a low cluster of 4- to 8-inch long leaves that are dark green with white along the middle of the leaf. Flower stalks with small white flowers develop from the crown. Plantlets also develop on the flower stalks. Indoors, this plant does best in moderate temperatures, medium light, and with moist soils.

Cordyline is often called *Dracaena* because of the similar appearance. Cordyline is treelike with long, more highly colored, and wider leaves. *Cordyline terminalis* has bronze-red foliage. This does best in high light intensities with moist soils. Several variegations are available.

- 'Red Dracaena,' coppery green shading to red foliage.
- 'Baby Ti,' dwarf plant with copper coloring, red margins on the foliage.
- 'Ti,' broad green foliage. The Hawaiian ti is used for grass skirts, floral arrangements, and other purposes. It is considered by Polynesians to be able to ward off evil spirits and to bring good luck.

The dragon lilies, *Dracaena*, may form large trees with woody stems topped with a crown of long leaves. The stems may often twist and branch into picturesque shapes. Dracaenas are well adapted to low light conditions. They may be grown with the roots in water alone. They look best at medium light with a moist soil.

Dracaena deremensis 'Warneckii,' the striped dracaena, has leaves with milky green center stripes and white stripes near the edge of the leaf; it is an excellent plant for air-conditioned rooms.

Dracaena fragrans 'Massangeana,' the corn plant, has leaves that arch and are striped light green and yellow down the middle of the leaf. This plant requires a lot of water. *Dracaena surculosa (D. godseffiana)*, the gold dust dracaena, has elliptical leaves in pairs or threes, spotted with yellow spots, and it is a small plant. The yellow spots become white with age. White fragrant flowers open at night.

'Florida Beauty' (*D. godseffiana* 'Florida Beauty') has more richly var-iegated leaves than the species. *Dracaena marginata* has red-edged leaves to 15 inches long. The canes twist in a picturesque fashion. Tolerant of low light, the older leaves fall if the soil is dry. *Dracaena sanderana*, the ribbon plant, has somewhat twisted, small leaves, green with broad white bands near the edge. *Dracaena sanderana borinquensis* has a milky green center and thin white stripes.

'Mondo grass,' *Ophiopogon japonicus*, forms a dense, bright green turf. A black form is available. The plant performs best at medium light and moist soils.

Sansevieria, the snake plants, are a source of commercial hemp. The thick leaves form a rosette and may be up to 4 feet long. Medium to high light intensities and a dry soil are best for these plants. *Sansevieria trifasciata* 'Hahnii,' the bird's-nest sansevieria, discovered in New Orleans, forms a small vaselike rosette of flattened leaves. *Sansevieria trifasciata* 'Laurentii,' the variegated snake plant, has yellow margins on the leaves.

ARROWROOT FAMILY (MARANTACEAE)

Named for a sixteenth-century botanist and physician, Maranti, these plants are mostly herbs from tropical America. While the rhizomes of some are used for food, the chief use is for ornamental purposes.

The peacock plant, *Calathea makoyana*, is one of the species of cala-thea that is prized for its colorful foliage. The foliage is thin and the plant has underground rhizomes. This plant should be kept in medium to high light, but out of direct sunlight. The soil should be moist.

Prayer plants *(Maranta)*, so named because the leaves fold lengthwise at evening and resemble hands in prayer, are used for their colorful foli-age. These plants are quite attractive if kept in moist soil in medium light. During mid-winter the plants take a rest; water only sparingly at this time.

Maranta leuconeura 'Erythroneura,' the red-veined prayer plant, has red veins as well as the olive green blotches. The underside of the leaf is red in color.

M. leuconeura 'Kerchoviana,' the prayer plant, has chocolate brown spots with red blotches beneath.

MULBERRY FAMILY (MORACEAE)

A rich mixture of uses has been the legacy of this family: food (fig, breadfruit), fodder, food for silkworms (leaves of various mulberries), medicine, beer flavoring (hops), fiber, and dyes. Commercial rubber can be made from the milky sap of *Ficus elastica*. Some of the other figs or banyan trees have figured in Eastern religion and legend.

The rubber plants, banyan, or figs are species of *Ficus*, one of the largest genus of plants. Among the famous plants are the ones under which Alexander's troops camped and the one that sheltered Robert Louis Stevenson in the banyan court in Honolulu, Hawaii. Medium light intensity and moist soils are best.

The weeping fig, *Ficus benjamina*, is one of the small-leaf tree forms of fig with weeping branches. The India rubber plant, *Ficus elastica*, is an old-time favorite. The species has been replaced by some newer cultivars, such as *F. elastica* 'Decora,' which has larger and broader leaves with a red underside. Fiddleleaf figs, *Ficus lyrata*, are another old-time favorite with large, 1- to 2-foot long, fiddle-shaped leaves.

MYRSINE FAMILY (MYRSINACEAE)

Named after the Greek name for myrrh, the plants in this family have little economic use except as plants in the human environment. As ornamental plants, many are excellent both indoors and outdoors.

Ardisia crenata, the coral berry, forms a small tree-shaped plant to about 4 feet tall. The fragrant white (often with a reddish tint) flowers and the persistent (up to 6 months) scarlet berries are, in addition to the glossy green foliage, considered when the coral berry is used indoors. The plant may become leggy, that is, devoid of lower foliage and shoots so the stem may be seen. To correct the leggy appearance, one may prune the coral berry; it responds well. Closely related to coral berry is the marlberry, *Ardisia japonica*. This plant is shorter, to 1½ feet, and tends to form a clump; all the leaves remain clustered at the end of the shoot. The small white flowers and small red berries remain hidden beneath the leaves as one looks down at the plant. The marlberry grows at a slow pace. Both coral berry and marlberry should be placed where they receive medium light intensity. The soil should be moist.

SCREW PINES (PANDANACEAE)

These plants resemble the *Dracaena*, trees with long, sword-shaped leaves crowning the stems. The plants with age develop stiltlike aerial roots to give the plant an appearance of being held upright by a number of slender stilts.

The variegated screw pine, *Pandanus veitchii*, does well indoors when placed in medium light and grown in dry soil. At each watering, however, the soil must be thoroughly soaked. The long, wide leaves (up to 3 inches wide) taper to a long point and recurve gracefully. Broad white margins and green middle sections are the leaf colors of value for indoor environments. Most pandanus leaves have very rough edges, so care should be exercised when placing them.

PALMS (PALMACEAE)

After the grasses, palms (named after the open palm of a hand) are the most useful of all plants for people. Often called king of plants, almost every human need from food to ornamentation may be satisfied by one or another palm. Every species may be useful in some manner: fiber; wood for shelters; leaves to thatch roofs, make mats, hats, and other items; food; oil; basic ingredient for sculptures; and medicine. Some of the more widely recognized palms are the coconut, date, and oil palms. The seeds of the palm *Phytelephas macrocarpa* have a hard ivorylike endosperm; it is called vegetable ivory and is used for carving.

Dwarf mountain palms (*Chamaedorea* species) are small palms, often with clustered stems, that are well adapted to poor indoor light conditions. They need moist soils. They are found naturally in the shade; the plants are relatively small, growing to 8 feet at maturity. The species from Mexico grow quite rapidly. *Chamaedorea elegans* 'Bella' from East Guatemala is a slower growing, dwarf form, reaching only 3 feet at maturity. Both of these plants are often sold as the neanthe bella palm; they appear very much alike.

Kentia palm, *Howea Forsterana*, is one of the specimens for indoor use. A native of the Lord Howe Islands east of Australia, this palm withstands tremendous amounts of abuse while indoors. As a result, it is the most commonly seen large specimen palm in interior environments. Giving the plant moist soils is best for plant appearance.

Lady palms or lady finger palms, *Rhapis excelsa*, are slow-growing palms that form clumps. In addition to the fingerlike segments of the dark green leaf, the coarse brown fibers that cover the stems have decorative value. These plants should be given medium light and the soil should be maintained dry.

PEPPER FAMILY (PIPERACEAE)

As the name implies, from this family comes spices. Actually, black and white pepper come from the same plant, *Piper nigrum*, the difference being in the ripeness of the fruit. Black pepper is extracted from immature fruit, white pepper from the mature fruit. In addition to spices, other uses have been for medicinal purposes and some salad greens.

All the pepcromias suffer (they are subject to rot) when the soil is kept moist to wet. They do much better when the soil is dry. As a group they are also tolerant of low light conditions. Peperomias may be divided into three groups by growth habit: upright, prostrate creeping, and essentially stemless clumps of leaves. The creeping forms are not seen as often as the others.

Oval-leaf peperomia, *P. obtusifolia*, and the variegated oval-leaf peperomia, *P. obtusifolia* 'Variegata,' are upright growers with succulent oval-shaped leaves. The stems are fleshy and the leaf is curved downward (concave).

Princess Astrid peperomia, *P. orba*, is a small-leafed bushy plant with the stem spotted red and white. This plant was discovered in a greenhouse in Sweden. Watermelon peperomia, *P. argyreia*, has an oval-shaped leaf with alternate silver and green bands much like those on some watermelons. The leaves arise from a short, stubby stem giving a stemless appearance.

Peperomia caperata has a heart-shaped leaf that is corrugated and quilted. All leaves arise from a short, stubby stem. Many variations are commonly seen. Among the best is the cultivar 'Emerald Ripple' with a chocolate tint in the valleys on the upper surface of the leaf and a pink petiole with red stripes.

JAPANESE YEWS (PODOCARPACEAE)

Woody, coniferous (cone-bearing) evergreens that are hardy in the warmer sections, these plants with flattened needlelike leaves may be used as small or large specimens and in combination with other plants in dish gardens. All are easily trained into bonsai plants. All should be placed in high light conditions and the soil maintained moist.

Weeping podocarpus, *Podocarpus gracilior*, has pendulous stems and soft narrow leaves that droop. Japanese yew, *Podocarpus macrophyllus*, maintains an upright growth with the leaves held horizontally. Broadleaf podocarpus, *Podocarpus Nagi*, has the widest leaf of all podocarpus. The stems are purplish, and the plant may weep.

FERNS (POLYPODIACEAE)

The name comes from the term signifying many feet and alludes to the branched rootstock of some species. Polypodiaceae is the largest of the fern families. Variation in growth habit is wide, from the walking fern that roots and forms plantlets whenever the tip of a frond touches the ground to the epiphytic staghorn ferns. A few of the ferns are used for food (young fronds or starchy rootstock); most are used for ornamental purposes, for cut fronds for floral arrangements, as well as for indoor and outdoor plantings.

Adiantum sp., maidenhair ferns, are small, dainty plants that require humid atmospheres for most attractive appearance. The fronds have a blackish wirelike stalk.

Asplenium sp. are collectively known as the spleenworts. A characteristic of some of the species is the formation of plantlets on the fronds. Moist soil, medium light intensity, and a humid atmosphere are required for best appearance.

Mother spleenwort, A. *bulbiferum*, is one of the species where plantlets form on older fronds. The long fronds (to 3 feet) may divide two or three times. The black leaf stalk is grooved. Bird's-nest fern, A. *nidus*, has long, undivided fronds that form a rosette. The midrib is black and the margins are wavy.

Holly fern, *Cyrtomium falcatum*, is one of the small ferns in the genus *Cyrtomium*. This group has leathery leaves and tolerates considerable abuse, including dry soil. Moist soil, low to medium light, and moderate temperatures are preferred. Plants are often sold under the name *Aspidium*. Fronds of the holly fern with a brown scaly stalk may reach a length of 2 feet.

Sword ferns, *Nephrolepis*, develop leaves from a crown, where they also develop their wirelike runners on which new plants form. The best known of these ferns is the Boston fern *Nephrolepis exaltata* 'Bostoniensis' and its many cultivars. As the name implies, the fern was found in Boston during the late 1800s. This fern does well indoors under adverse conditions; moist soils and medium light conditions should be given where possible. Among the outstanding cultivars are 'Fluffy Ruffles,' a dwarf cultivar, the fronds of which are finely divided and about 12 inches long, and 'Whitmanii' with fronds to 18 inches long, arching or hanging downward with evenly cut segments.

Staghorn ferns, *Platycerium* sp., named for the strangely divided antlerlike leaf, are epiphytes with two types of leaves, the green divided fronds arising from a pad of brownish leaves. Beneath the brown leaves are the roots that hold the plant on the tree. Staghorn ferns are usually grown on bark to be used as hanging plants against a wall. *Platycerium bifurcatum* is probably the most tolerant species for indoor environments. It also is rather tolerant of cold. The best conditions would be medium light with the bark, or moss, under the pad kept moist.

The table ferns are species and cultivars of the genus *Pteris*. Small plants, table ferns are used in dish gardens, terrariums, and as a small specimen. As a group, this group of ferns is quite tolerant of indoor conditions. They should be given medium light intensities and the soil kept moist. Repotting the plants is necessary for maximum attractiveness. The silver table fern, *P. ensiformis* 'Victoriae,' is an outstanding example. Green with white bands and wavy margins, the fronds are up to 14 inches long.

ROSE FAMILY (ROSACEAE)

Many of the most important fruits are members of the rose family: apple, pear, quince, cherry, and strawberry, to mention a few. Many other products come from the rose family: oils, perfumes, medicine, and wines.

The loquat *Eriobotrya japonica* is an important evergreen ornamental plant for the garden that adapts well to indoor conditions. For the best performance, moist soils and high light intensities are needed. Many varieties have been developed for the edible fruit, which probably will not develop indoors.

SAXIFRAGE FAMILY (SAXIFRAGACEAE)

The name of the saxifrage family is from Latin signifying the breaking of rock. This alludes to the fact that many species of the family grow in nature in clefts of rock. Representatives grow from the tropics to the arctics. Among the uses has been that of using the rough leaves of *Deutzia scabra* to polish wood.

Strawberry begonia is neither strawberry nor begonia, but *Saxifraga stolonifera* (S. *sarmentosa*). From the cluster of leaves, runners form during the summer on which new plants form. 'Tricolor' is an attractive cultivar with green, white, and pink leaves. High light intensities are necessary for the best color development. The soil should be moist.

NETTLES (URTICACEAE)

Many species of this family are covered with spiny hair that contain formic acid, which causes a stinging sensation when touched. Thus the name from the Latin, which signifies to burn. The plants used indoors do not sting.

Trailing watermelon begonia, *Pellionia daveauana*, is a trailing plant with succulent pinkish stems. The satin pellionia, *P. pulchra*, has grayish leaves with darker veins that are purplish beneath. Both of these plants should be placed in high light and the soils should be moist.

Pilea cadierei has been called the aluminum plant because of the silvery aluminum marking on the foliage. A rather rapid grower, the plant becomes leggy, but responds well to pruning to maintain compact plants. Medium light intensities with a moist soil should be maintained.

Friendship plants, *Pilea involucrata*, have ascending branches and closely packed, oval, deeply quilted leaves. The light intensity influences the color from deep green in low light to coppery red-brown at higher intensities. The underside is wine red. Indoors, medium light and moist soils would be preferred.

Pilea Silver Tree has silver bands on the leaf. Underside of the leaf is reddish. Moist soil and medium light intensity are preferred.

GRAPE FAMILY (VITACEAE)

Mostly vines, this family has distinctive berries. Well known is the grape, *Vitis*, for table and for wine. *Cissus* is the genus of several important indoor plants. The names of these plants are often confused and the genera names *Vitis* and *Rhiocissus* are often used.

The kangaroo vine is *Cissus antarctica*, often sold as *Rhiocissus antarctica*. This plant grows rapidly, is excellent indoors, tolerating warm locations or air conditioning. It is best at medium to high light and with a moist soil.

The grape ivy is *Cissus rhombifolia*; it may be found as *Vitis rhombifolia*. Each leaf is composed of three diamond-shaped leaflets. Dry soil should be the rule for this plant.

The following tables provide guides to the use of plants under various indoor conditions.

TABLE 7–1
Plants Well Adapted to Indoor Environments

An "average" environment does not exist, because light conditions and air movement vary from one place to another. However, some plants, given reasonable care, look better than others when grown inside. The following are some of the plants that adapt well. They are easily obtained. The listing also reflects the rich variations possible for indoor environments.

SCIENTIFIC NAME	COMMON NAME
Acorus gramineus 'Variegatus'	Miniature sweet flag
Aechmea fasciata	Silvervase
Aglaonema commutatum var. *maculatum*	Silver evergreen
Aglaonema commutatum 'White Rajah'	Golden evergreen
Aglaonema modestum	Chinese evergreen
Araucaria heterophylla	Norfolk Island pine
Ardisia crenata	Coral berry
Ardisia japonica	Marlberry
Asparagus setaceus	Asparagus fern
Asparagus densiflorus 'Myers'	Plume asparagus
Asparagus densiflorus cv. 'Sprengeri'	Sprengeri fern
Aspidistra elatior	Cast-iron plant
Aspidistra elatior 'Variegata'	Variegated cast-iron plant
Aucuba japonica 'Variegata'	Gold-dust plant
Begonia x Cleopatra	—
Brassaia actinophylla	Schefflera
Chamaedorea elegans	Dwarf mountain palm
Chamaedorea elegans 'Bella'	Neanthe bella palm
Chlorophytum comosum 'Vittatum'	Spider plant
Cissus antarctica	Kangaroo vine
Cissus rhombifolia	Grape ivy
Cissus rhombifolia 'Mandaiana'	—
Crassula argentea	Jade plant
Cyrtomium falcatum	Holly fern
Dieffenbachia amoena	Giant dumbcane
Dieffenbachia 'Exotica'	—
Dieffenbachia picta 'Rudolph Roehrs'	—
Dieffenbachia picta 'Superba'	—
Dizygotheca elegantissima	Spider aralia
Dracaena deremensis 'Janet Craig'	—
Dracaena deremensis 'Warneckii'	Striped dracaena
Dracaena fragrans 'Massangeana'	Corn plant
Dracaena surculosa	Gold-dust dracaena
Dracaena marginata	—
Dracaena sanderana	Ribbon plant

(continued on following page)

TABLE 7–1 (Continued)

SCIENTIFIC NAME	COMMON NAME
Dracaena sanderana 'borinquensis'	—
Epipremnum aureum	Devil's ivy
Fatshedera lizei	—
Fatsia japonica	—
Ficus benjamina	Weeping fig
Ficus elastica	India rubber plant
Ficus elastica 'Decora'	—
Ficus lyrata	Fiddleleaf fig
Hedera helix varieties	English ivy
Howea forsterana	Kentia palm
Hoya carnosa	Wax plant
Hoya carnosa 'Variegata'	Variegated wax plant
Maranta leuconeura 'Erythroneura'	Red-veined prayer plant
Maranta leuconeura 'Kerchoviana'	Prayer plant
Monstera deliciosa	Ceriman
Nephrolepis exaltata 'Bostoniensis' varieties	Boston fern
Ophiopogon japonicus	Mondo grass
Pandanus Veitchii	Variegated screw pine
Peperomia caperata 'Emerald Ripple'	—
Peperomia obtusifolia	Oval-leaf peperomia
Peperomia obtusifolia 'Variegata'	—
Peperomia orba	Princess Astrid peperomia
Peperomia argyreia	Watermelon peperomia
Philodendron domesticum	—
Philodendron x 'Emerald Queen'	—
Philodendron scandens subsp. oxycardium	Heart-leaf philodendron
Philodendron panduriforme	Horsehead philodendron
Philodendron selloum	Lacy tree philodendron
Philodendron x 'Wend-imbe'	—
Pilea cadierei	Aluminum plant
Pilea involucrata	Friendship plant
Pilea Silver Tree	—
Platycerium bifurcatum	Staghorn fern
Plectranthus nummularius	Creeping Charlie
Podocarpus gracilior	Weeping podocarpus
Podocarpus macrophyllus	Japanese yew
Podocarpus Nagi	Broadleaf podocarpus
Polyscias balfouriana 'Marginata'	Variegated Balfour aralia
Pteris ensiformis 'Victoriae'	Silver table fern
Rhapis excelsa	Lady palm
Rhoeo spathacea	Moses in the cradle
Sansevieria trifasciata	Snake plant

TABLE 7–1 (Continued)

SCIENTIFIC NAME	COMMON NAME
Sansevieria trifasciata 'Hahnii'	Bird's-nest sansevieria
Sansevieria trifasciata 'Laurentii'	Variegated snake plant
Saxifraga stolonifera 'Tricolor'	—
Spathiphyllum clevelandii	White flag
Spathiphyllum x 'Mauna Loa'	White anthurium
Syngonium podophyllum	Nephthytis
Syngonium augustatum 'albolineatum'	—
Syngonium podophyllum 'Trileaf Wonder'	—
Tradescantia fluminensis	Wandering Jew
Tupidanthus calyptratus	Mallet flower
Zebrina pendula	Silvery wandering Jew

TABLE 7–2
Plants for Special Conditions

ROOTS IN WATER

Although you cannot keep a soil mixture flooded with water and expect a plant to grow, you can grow several plants with their roots in tap water alone. Coarse gravel may be used for support, if desired, but soil and organic matter must be excluded from the base. Lumps of charcoal may be added to help keep the water fresh.

Either start new plants in water, or wash away the soil completely from the root system. Bubbling air through the water is not necessary.

Algae may grow in the water, on the roots, and on the side of the container. When this occurs, wash the roots and container. Algae grow faster in clear glass than in dark containers.

Some plants that do well in water are:

Aglaonema modestum (Chinese evergreen)
Cissus rhombifolia (grape ivy)
Crassula argentea (jade plant)
Dieffenbachia, all species and varieties (dumbcanes)
Dracaena sanderana
Epipremnum aureum (devil's ivy)
Fatshedera lizei
Hedera helix, all varieties (English ivy)
Philodendron scandens subsp. *oxycardium* (heart-leaf philodendron)
Philodendron panduriforme (horsehead philodendron)
Sansevieria, all varieties (snake plant)
Syngonium podophyllum varieties (nephthytis)
Tolmiea menziesii
Tradescantia fluminensis (wandering Jew)
Zebrina pendula (silvery wandering Jew)

(continued on following page)

TABLE 7–2 (Continued)

ADVERSE CONDITIONS

Some tough plants can withstand adverse indoor conditions, such as low light and high temperature, better than others. For such locations, consider these plants:

Aglaonema modestum (Chinese evergreen)

Aspidistra elatior (cast-iron plant)

Aucuba japonica 'Variegata' (gold-dust plant)

Brassaia actinophylla (schefflera)

Chamaedorea elegans (dwarf mountain palm)

Cissus rhombifolia (grape ivy)

Crassula argentea (jade plant)

Cyrtomium falcatum (holly fern)

Dieffenbachia amoena (giant dumbcane)

Dracaena fragrans 'massangeana' (corn plant)

Epipremnum aureum (devil's ivy)

Ficus elastica (India rubber plant)

Ficus lyrata (fiddleleaf fig)

Howea forsterana (Kentia palm)

Pandanus veitchii (variegated screw pine)

Peperomia obtusifolia (oval-leaf peperomia)

Philodendron scandens subsp. *oxycardium* (heart-leaf philodendron)

Podocarpus macrophyllus (Japanese yew)

Sansevieria, all varieties (snake plant)

Syngonium podophyllum (nephthytis)

PLANTS FOR HOT, DRY LOCATIONS

In addition to cactus and other succulents, plants that do well in hot and dry locations include:

Bromeliads, all varieties and species

Epipremnum aureum (devil's ivy)

Peperomia obtusifolia (oval-leaf peperomia)

Sansevieria, all varieties (snake plant)

Tradescantia fluminensis (wandering Jew)

PLANTS ADAPTED TO LOW LIGHT

Within the home or office, the most variable condition is light: intensity, color, and time of day and night when lights are on. We use plants to make environments for us, but the environment, particularly light, may not be suitable for the best health of plants. Naturally, if the plant fails, the mood of the room changes.

Plants can tolerate low light if you acclimate them to such areas by selecting the right varieties and watering them at infrequent intervals to prevent wilting. When you first introduce a plant into a low-light area, gradually lengthen the interval between waterings. A few older leaves may turn yellow and fall.

Do not fertilize these plants. Your objective is to keep them alive and looking well, not to have them grow larger. Therefore, start with plants of the desired size. Remove new growth that is not attractive or normal in appearance.

(continued)

TABLE 7–2 (Continued)

Some varieties are better able to survive in low light conditions. Consider these before trying others:

Aechmea fasciata (silvervase)
Aglaonema commutatum var. maculatum (silver evergreen)
Aglaonema commutatum 'White Rajah' (golden evergreen)
Aglaonema modestum (Chinese evergreen)
Araucaria heterophylla (Norfolk Island pine)
Aspidistra elatior (cast-iron plant)
Chamaedorea elegans (dwarf mountain palm)
Chamaedorea elegans 'Bella' (neanthe bella palm)
Crassula argentea (jade plant)
Dieffenbachia amoena (giant dumbcane)
Dracaena, all species and varieties

Epipremnum aureum (devil's ivy)
Ficus elastica 'Decora'
Howea forsterana (Kentia palm)
Hoya carnosa (wax plant)
Hoya carnosa 'Variegata' (variegated wax plant)
Monstera deliciosa (ceriman)
Pandanus veitchii (variegated screw pine)
Peperomia, all species and varieties
Philodendron, all species and varieties
Podocarpus macrophyllus (Japanese yew)
Sansevieria, all species and varieties

TABLE 7–3
Plants Somewhat Temperamental Indoors

SCIENTIFIC NAME	COMMON NAME
Adiantum decorum 'Pacific Mail'	—
Aeschynanthus pulcher	Royal red bugler
Anthurium scherzerianum	Flamingo flower
Aphelandra squarrosa 'Dania'	Zebra plant
Asplenium bulbiferum	Mother spleenwort
Asplenium nidus	Bird's-nest fern
Calathea makoyana	Peacock plant
Codiaeum variegatum var. pictum, 'Aucubifolium,' 'Elaine'	Aucuba leaf or goldspot croton Lanceleaf croton
Columnea	—
Cordyline terminalis, 'Red Draceana,' 'Baby Ti,' 'Ti'	—
Cycas revoluta	Sago palm
Episcia cupreata 'Acajou'	—
Eriobotrya japonica	Loquat
Fittonia verschaffeltii var. argyroneura	Nerve plant
Gynura aurantiaca	Velvet plant
Pellionia daveauana	Trailing watermelon begonia

Appendices

APPENDIX 1

Soil mixtures are used for indoor plantings. Whenever a soil mixture is not adequate in physical or chemical characteristics, changes must be made to insure easier maintenance and more healthy plantings.

The four major components of a soil mixture are:

- **Mineral (inorganic) matter:** Broken and weathered particles—sand, salt, and clay.

- **Organic matter:** Living and dead matter in various stages of decomposition. Humus is a gelatinous product that is quite resistant to decomposition, usually dark (brown or black) in color, colloidal in size, holds water and nutrient ions.

- **Soil water:** Held on the surface of particles in the soil and in the spaces between particles. Water held with various degrees of tenacity in the soil. Some of the water is not available for plant growth.

- **Air:** In the larger spaces between particles.

Important Manipulations and Treatments a Soil Mixture Must Withstand

CONSIDERATION	WHY IMPORTANT?
Compaction	During the potting and planting operation, the soil mixture is firmed around the roots of the soil to provide good support for the newly transplanted plant. The soil mixture should compact well but should resist overcompaction. Overcompaction will result in increased weight, (bulk density), reduced air porosity, and reduced water infiltration and conductivity rate. The levels reached may be detrimental to plant growth.
Heat treatment	Most soil mixtures are subjected to temperatures of 160°F. for 30 minutes or longer. The purpose of these treatments is to pasturize the soil for elimination of diseases, nematodes, and weed seeds contained in the components of the soil mixture. The components of the soil mix must withstand this treatment without change.
Stability	Physical properties of the soil mixture must remain fairly stable over a long period of time. Some components will change rapidly causing a rapid change in the physical properties as well. For example, some types of organic matter decompose rapidly, resulting in changing porosity and water movement characteristics. Chemical properties may also be affected in an adverse mature. For example, organic matter high in carbon and low in nitrogen, such as some sawdusts, uses nitrogen at the expense of the plant—thus additional nitrogen must be given. However, after an initial rapid decomposition and use of nitrogen, decomposition slows, resulting in a liberation of nitrogen that can be detrimental to plant growth. The liberation of nitrogen is caused by the death of the microorganisms that were rapidly decomposing the fresh organic matter.

(Continued on following pages)

Important Chemical Properties of Soil Mixtures

PROPERTY	WHAT IS MEASURED	WHY IMPORTANT	METHODS TO CHANGE
Cation Exchange Capacity (CEC)	Amount of positively charged ions held by soil and released to plants	Maintains a reserve of essential ions for plant growth. Provides buffering.	To increase, add organic matter such as peat moss.
Salinity	Total salts in soil	Excess amount injure plants, retards growth.	Flush out (leach) excess with water.
pH	Acidity of the soil	Acidity of soil and soil water influence availability of nutrients, growth of microorganism and plant roots.	To neutralize acidity, add lime and fertilizers such as calcium nitrate that leaves an alkaline residue. To acidify, add peat moss in soil mixture. Iron sulfate and ammonium nitrate will result in increased acidity when used over a period of time.

Important Physical Properties of Soil Mixtures

PROPERTY	WHAT IS MEASURED	WHY IMPORTANT	METHODS TO CHANGE
Bulk density	Weight of soil	Heavy soils increase cost of shipment of plants. Heavy soils may indicate poor physical condition of soil.	To lighten, incorporate organic matter and coarse aggregates.
Porosity	Spaces in soil containing air	Normal root growth and functioning require oxygen.	To increase, incorporate coarse aggregates and organic matter.
Infiltration and conductivity of water	How rapidly water enters and passes through a soil mixture.	Rapid movement necessary to avoid water logging.	Incorporate coarse aggregate and organic matter to increase.
Water retention	Water held by soil and available for plant growth	In part, frequency of irrigation influenced by water retention.	Incorporate organic matter to increase.

Appendix 1 / 159

Procedures for Correcting Problems Encountered
with Soil Mixtures

PROBLEMS	CORRECTION
Poor infiltration and water movement in soil mixture.	• Increase porosity by incorporating coarse inorganic or organic matter at at least 30% by volume. • Do not compact soil mixture at planting. • Work soil only at proper moisture content. • Correct irrigation practices to avoid soil compaction during irrigating.
Not enough water retained.	• Increase water holding capacity by incorporating more organic matter.
Soil mix too heavy.	• Reduce weight by incorporating light-weight aggregated or organic matter or both. Use at least 30% volume of each component of the soil mixture.
Poor aeration.	• Incorporate coarse particles of organic matter. • Do not compact soil during planting. • Proper irrigation procedures to eliminate compaction of soil during irrigation. • Work soil only at proper moisture content.
Herbicide toxicity.	• Find clean source of all components of the soil mixture. • Incorporating activated charcoal will reduce toxicity. As much as 1.5 pounds per cubic yard may be needed.

APPENDIX 2

Over the years, many types of soil mixtures were used by growers of plants for interior landscapes. Because of the necessity of adapting cultural practices to the soil mixture, attempts were made to develop standardized mixtures that would have the same chemical and physical properties batch after batch. The principle mixtures and a description of them are described below.

John Innis Composts.   These are based on the use of clay loam soils of a defined nature. To this is added peat and a very coarse sand. Different proportions are used depending on the intended use of the compost. Typical are

- *Seed:* 2 parts loam, 1 part peat, 1 part sand with 2 lbs. superphosphate and 1 lb. calcium carbonate added to each cubic yard.

- *Potting:* 7 parts loam, 3 parts peat, 2 parts sand with 2 lbs. horn and hoof, 2 lbs. superphosphate, 1 lb. potassium sulphate, and 1 lb. calcium carbonate to each cubic yard.

The UC System.   This is a system of soil mixtures and fertilizer incorporations and additions based on the use of a sand of a defined characteristic and mixing with peat moss.

This was the further refinement of loamless soil mixtures, research on which began many years ago. In the 1920's and 1930's Alex Laurie in Ohio studied the use of peat-sand mixtures. The UC system imployed the systems concept of defining the characteristics of the sand and the peat used, and the fertilization necessary for well-grown plants. Other aspects of soil pasturization, materials handling, etc., was also included as part of the system.

The specifications for the sand are as follows:

- Coarse sand (0.5 to 1.0 mm)—not to exceed 12% to 15%

- Fine sand (0.1 to 0.25 mm)—At least 70% and preferably 85%.

- Salt and clay (less than 0.05 mm)—not to exceed 15%, preferably much less.

The peat moss should be sphagnum peat of the coarse, horticultural grade.

In the years following the introduction of the entire concept, other types of organic matter have been substituted for the peat moss. Most notably has been redwood sawdust. Some people claim that the sand-redwood sawdust is not a UC system soil mixture—others dispute this.

Over the years, many substitutions have been used in the original UC concept. Most of the substitutions have resulted in soil mixtures of inadequate physical characteristics—reverting to the original problems the UC concept was designed to eliminate. These problems are inadequate aeration of the soil mixture, difficulty in leaching excess salts, and root diseases that are difficult to control.

Sand-Bark.   Because of the difficulties with inadequate porosity found in many so-called UC mixes, coarsely ground bark has been substituted for the peat moss and for the sawdust. The large particle sizes and the long lasting characteristic of bark resulted in soil mixtures with 25% air-filled porosity that was stable for many months. These soils drain rapidly and are not limiting in the amount of oxygen available to the plant roots. Results have been easier control of root diseases.

Cornell Peat-lite.   This was a further refinement of a totally loamless soil mixture studied in Texas by A. F. DeWorth. The concept uses perlite, peat moss, and vermiculite in varying proportions. Various preplant and postplant fertilization programs are possible. Peatlite mixes are used primarily for bedding plants and for potted plants grown in greenhouses.

Recent alterations of the concept is to substitute plastic particles (foam, beads, etc.) for some or all of the perlite. Depending on the intended crop, various sizes or grades of the various components are used.

Water and soil analysis to determine their chemical composition is used by all horticulturists. Intrepretation of the results is more important than the routine running of the tests. Guidelines to understanding the results are described on the following pages.

Interpretation of Water Analysis

Should be considered in relation to other observations and analysis such as soil and leaf analysis.

TEST	HOW REPORTED	GENERAL INTERPRETATIONS
Salinity (Salt content)	EC (millimhos)	Measure of hazard from salinity. • Below 0.5—Low salt content may cause permeability problem. • Below 0.75—Low hazard, used for most crops. • 0.75–1.5—Medium. Use for moderately tolerant crops. • 1.5–3.0—High hazard. Use only for highly tolerant crops. Note: To convert to ppm, multiply EC by 640.
Boron	B (ppm)	Measure of boron toxicity potential. • Below 0.5—Satisfactory for all crops. • 0.5–1.0—Sensitive crops may show injury. • 1.0–2.0—Sensitive crops injured. Good for semi-tolerant crops. • 2.0–4.0—Use only for tolerant crops. • Above 4.0—Unsatisfactory for crops.
Chlorides	Cl (me/l)	Many ornamentals are sensitive to Chlorides. • Below 2—Satisfactory. • 2.0 to 10—Sensitive crops show leaf burn. • Above 10—Generally unsatisfactory. Note: Constantly wetting leaves of plants with water containing 3.0 me/l of Cl or Na can cause defoliation or leaf burn.
Calcium plus magnesium	Ca + Mg (me/l)	In formula to calculate Sodium Absorption Ratio.
Sodium	Na (me/l)	In formula to calculate SAR.

Sodium Absorption Ratio	SAR	Calculated value as follows:

$$SAR = Na \div \frac{Ca + Mg}{2}$$

Used to estimate Exchangeable Sodium Percentage (ESP) in soil after long-time use of water for irrigation.

SAR (water)	ESP (soil)	Interpretation
Below 6	Below 10	No permeability problem.
6–9	10–15	Possible problem in fine textured soils (SP above 50).
Above 9	Above 15	Permeability problem. Likely except for sandy soils (SP below 20).

Acidity	pH	Alkaline irrigation waters adversely affect some crops.
Carbonates plus Bicarbonates	$CO_3 + HCO_3$ (me/l)	Calcium deposits may clog nozzles, deposits on leaves objectionable. Require acid treatment to eliminate. Phosphoric acid used because of safety.
Nitrates	$NO_3 - N$ (ppm)	Calculate in determining fertilization additions. Conversions:

- $NO_3 - N \times 2.72 = N$ in lbs/ac. ft. of water
- $NO_3 - N \times 4.4 = NO_3$ in ppm
- $NO_3 - N \times .0714 = N$ in me/l

APPENDIX 4

Often the information we need is not in convenient terms. Conversion from one form to another is necessary. On the following pages are the more common conversions horticulturists will be making.

TYPE OF CONVERSION	MULTIPLY	BY	TO OBTAIN
	Milliequivalents	*Equivalent weight*	*Milligrams*
Milliequivalents to milligrams	Ca	20.04	Ca
	Mg	12.16	Mg
	Na	23.00	Na
	K	39.10	K
	Cl	35.46	Cl
	SO_4	48.03	SO_4
	CO_3	30.00	CO_3
	HCO_3	61.01	HCO_3
	PO_4	31.65	PO_4
	$CaSO_4 \cdot 2H_2O$	86.09	$CaSO_4 \cdot 2H_2O$
	$CaCO_3$	50.04	$CaCO_3$
	S	16.03	S
	H_2SO_4	49.04	H_2SO_4
	$Al_2(SO_4)_3 \cdot 18H_2O$	111.07	$Al_2(SO_4)_3 \cdot 18H_2O$
	$FeSO_4 \cdot 7H_2O$	139.01	$FeSo_4 \cdot 7H_2O$

	Milliequivalents per liter	*Equivalent weight*	*Parts per million*
Milliequivalents per liter to parts per million	Ca	20.04	Ca
	Mg	12.16	Mg
	Na	23.00	Na
	K	39.10	K
	Cl	35.46	Cl
	SO_4	48.03	SO_4
	CO_3	30.00	CO_3
	HCO_3	61.01	HCO_3
	PO_4	31.65	PO_4
	$CaSO_4 \cdot 2H_2O$	86.09	$CaSO_4 \cdot 2H_2O$
	$CaCO_3$	50.04	$CaCo_3$
	S	16.03	S
	H_2SO_4	49.04	H_2SO_4
	$Al_2(SO_4)_3 \cdot 18H_2O$	111.07	$Al_2(SO_4)_3 \cdot 18H_2O$
	$FeSO_4 \cdot 7H_2O$	139.01	$FeSO_4 \cdot 7H_2O$

(Continued on following pages)

TYPE OF CONVERSION	MULTIPLY	BY		TO OBTAIN
	Milliequivalents per liter of saturation extract	Equivalent weight	$\times \dfrac{\% H_2O \text{ in soil at saturation}}{100}$	Parts per million in dry soil
Milliequivalents per liter of saturation extract to parts per million in dry soil	Ca	20.04	$\times \dfrac{\% H_2O}{100}$	Ca
	Mg	12.16	$\times \dfrac{\% H_2O}{100}$	Mg
	Na	23.00	$\times \dfrac{\% H_2O}{100}$	Na
	K	39.10	$\times \dfrac{\% H_2O}{100}$	K
	Cl	35.46	$\times \dfrac{\% H_2O}{100}$	Cl
	SO_4	48.03	$\times \dfrac{\% H_2O}{100}$	SO_4
	CO_3	30.00	$\times \dfrac{\% H_2O}{100}$	CO_3
	HCO_3	61.01	$\times \dfrac{\% H_2O}{100}$	HCO_3
	PO_4	31.65	$\times \dfrac{\% H_2O}{100}$	PO_4
	$CaSO_4 \cdot 2H_2O$	86.09	$\times \dfrac{\% H_2O}{100}$	$CaSO_4 \cdot 2H_2O$
	$CaCO_3$	50.04	$\times \dfrac{\% H_2O}{100}$	$CaCO_3$
	S	16.03	$\times \dfrac{\% H_2O}{100}$	S
	H_2SO_4	49.04	$\times \dfrac{\% H_2O}{100}$	H_2SO_4
	$Al_2(SO_4)_3 \cdot 18H_2O$	111.07	$\times \dfrac{\% H_2O}{100}$	$Al_2(SO_4)_3 \cdot 18H_2O$
	$FeSO_4 \cdot 7H_2O$	139.01	$\times \dfrac{\% H_2O}{100}$	$FeSO_4 \cdot 7H_2O$

TO CONVERT	MULTIPLY	BY (decimals omitted)	TO OBTAIN
	Milliequivalents per 100 grams of soil	*Equivalent weight × 20*	*Pounds per acre 0″–6″*
Milliequivalents per 100 grams of soil to pounds per acre 0″–6″ (assuming 2,000,000 pounds of soil per acre 6 inches)	Ca	400	Ca
	Mg	243	Mg
	Na	460	Na
	K	782	K
	Cl	710	Cl
	HCO_3	1220	HCO_3
	CO_3	600	CO_3
	SO_4	960	SO_4
	NO_3	1240	NO_3
	$CaSO_4 \cdot 2H_2O$	1721	$CaSO_4 \cdot 2H_2O$
	$CaCO_3$	1000	$CaCO_3$

TYPE OF CONVERSION	MULTIPLY	BY	TO OBTAIN
Volume units	Milliliters	6.102×10^{-2}	Cubic inches
	Milliliters	1×10^{-6}	Cubic meters
	Milliliters	3.53×10^{-5}	Cubic feet
	Milliliters	2.642×10^{-4}	Gallons
	Milliliters	10^{-3}	Liters
	Milliliters	1.057×10^{-3}	Quarts, liquid
	Milliliters	0.034	Fluid ounces
	Cubic feet	2.832×10^{4}	Cubic centimeters
	Cubic feet	1728	Cubic inches
	Cubic feet	0.03704	Cubic yards
	Cubic feet	7.48052	Gallons
	Cubic feet	28.32	Liters
	Cubic feet	0.23743	Barrels (U.S.)
	Cubic inches	16.39	Cubic centimeters
	Cubic inches	5.787×10^{-4}	Cubic feet
	Cubic inches	4.329×10^{-3}	Gallons
	Cubic inches	1.639×10^{-2}	Liters

(Continued on following pages)

TYPE OF CONVERSION	MULTIPLY	BY	TO OBTAIN
Volume units (Continued)	Cubic meters	35.31	Cubic feet
	Cubic meters	1.308	Cubic yards
	Cubic meters	264.2	Gallons
	Cubic yards	27	Cubic feet
	Cubic yards	0.7646	Cubic meters
	Cubic yards	202.0	Gallons
	Gallons (U.S.)	231.0	Cubic inches
	Gallons (U.S.)	3785	Cubic centimeters
	Gallons (U.S.)	0.1337	Cubic feet
	Gallons (U.S.)	3.785	Liters
	Gallons (U.S.)	0.83267	Imperial gallons
	Gallons (U.S.)	128	Fluid ounces
	Liters	0.03531	Cubic feet
	Liters	61.02	Cubic inches
	Liters	0.2642	Gallons
	Liters	33.8	Fluid ounces
	Acre-inches	3630	Cubic feet
	Acre-inches	27,167	Gallons
	Acre-inches	0.0833	Acre-feet
	Acre-feet	43,560	Cubic feet
	Acre-feet	326,000	Gallons
	Acre-feet	12	Acre-inches
	Each 1000 gallons	133.7	Cubic feet
	Bushel	1.2444	Cubic feet
	Bushel	32	Quarts (dry)
	Bushel	35.238	Liters

TYPE OF CONVERSION	MULTIPLY	BY	TO OBTAIN
Area units	Acre	43,560	Square feet
	Acre	0.0015625	Square miles
	Acre	4840	Square yards
	Acre	0.40468	Hectare
	Acre	4046.8	Square meters
	Acre	160	Square rods

TYPE OF CONVERSION	MULTIPLY	BY	TO OBTAIN
Area units (Continued)	Hectare	2.471	Acres (U.S.)
	Hectare	10,000	Square meters
	Square feet (U.S.)	144	Square inches
	Square feet (U.S.)	929.034	Square centimeters
	Square inches (U.S.)	645.16	Square millimeters
	Square inches (U.S.)	6.4516	Square centimeters
	Square mile	640	Acres
	Square mile	258.99	Hectares
	Square yard	9	Square feet
	Square yard	0.83613	Square meter

TYPE OF CONVERSION	MULTIPLY	BY	TO OBTAIN
Weight units	Tons (long)	1.12	Tons (short)
	Tons (long)	2240	Pounds
	Tons (long)	1016.047	Kilograms
	Tons (short)	2000	Pounds
	Tons (short)	907.1848	Kilograms
	Tons (short)	0.90718	Tons (metric)
	Tons (metric)	2205	Pounds
	Tons (metric)	1000	Kilograms
	Cubic feet water	62.43	Pounds water
	Acre-feet water	2.72×10^6	Pounds water
	Acre-feet soil	4.0×10^6	Pounds soil (approx.)
	Cubic feet soil	68 to 112	Pounds soil
	Gallons water	8.3453	Pounds water
	Grains (Troy)	0.0648	Grams

(Continued on following pages)

TYPE OF CONVERSION	MULTIPLY	BY	TO OBTAIN
Weight units (Continued)	Grams	15.43	Grains
	Grams	10^3	Milligrams
	Grams	0.03527	Ounces
	Grams	2205×10^{-3}	Pounds
	Kilograms	2.205	Pounds
	Ounces	16	Drams
	Ounces	0.0625	Pounds
	Ounces	28.3495	Grams
	Ounces (Troy)	480	Grains
	Ounces (Troy)	31.10348	Grams
	Pounds	16	Ounces
	Pounds	7000	Grains
	Pounds	0.0005	Tons (short)
	Pounds	453.5924	Grams
	Pounds	14.5833	Ounces (Troy)
	Pounds water	0.01602	Cubic feet water
	Pounds water	27.68	Cubic inches
	Pounds water	0.1198	Gallons
	Pounds per acre	0.00124	Pounds per cubic yard
	Pounds per acre	.0023	Pounds per 1000 square foot

TYPE OF CONVERSION	MULTIPLY	BY	TO OBTAIN
Pressure units	Atmospheres	76.0	Centimeters mercury
	Atmospheres	29.92	Inches mercury
	Atmospheres	33.90	Feet water
	Atmospheres	1.0333	Kilograms per square centimeter
	Atmospheres	14.70	Pounds per square inch
	Atmospheres	1.058	Tons per square foot
	Centimeters mercury	0.01316	Atmospheres
	Centimeters mercury	0.1934	Pounds per square inch

TYPE OF CONVERSION	MULTIPLY	BY	TO OBTAIN
Pressure units (Continued)	Bar	0.9869	Atmospheres
	Feet water	0.02950	Atmospheres
	Feet water	0.8826	Inches mercury
	Feet water	62.43	Pounds per square foot
	Inches mercury	0.03342	Atmospheres
	Inches mercury	1.133	Feet water
	Inches mercury	70.73	Pounds per square foot
	Inches water	0.002458	Atmospheres
	Inches water	0.07355	Inches mercury
	Pounds per square inch	0.06804	Atmospheres
	Pounds per square inch	2.036	Inches mercury
Rate of flow units	Cubic feet per second	448.8	Gallons per minute
	Cubic feet per second	0.646	Million gallons per day
	Cubic feet per second	50.0	So. Calif. miner's inches
	Cubic feet per second	40.0	Calif. statute miner's inches
	Cubic feet per second	23.8	Acre-inches per 24 hours
	Cubic feet per second	1.984	Acre-feet per 24 hours
	Gallons per minute	0.00223	Cubic feet per second
	Gallons per minute	0.00144	Million gallons per day
	Gallons per minute	0.114	So. Calif. miner's inches
	Gallons per minute	0.053	Acre-inches per 24 hours
	So. Calif. miner's inches	8.98	Gallons per minute
	So. Calif. miner's inches	0.476	Acre-inches per 24 hours
	So. Calif. miner's inches	0.80	Calif. statute miner's inches
	Acre-inches in 24 hours	2.10	So. Calif. miner's inches
	Acre-inches in 24 hours	18.86	Gallons per minute
	Acre-inches in 24 hours	0.042	Cubic feet per second
	Million gallons per day	1.547	Cubic feet per second
	Million gallons per day	694.4	Gallons per minute
	Million gallons per day	77.36	So. Calif. miner's inches
	Million gallons per day	36.81	Acre-inches in 24 hours

(Continued on following page)

TYPE OF CONVERSION	MULTIPLY	BY	TO OBTAIN
Temperature units	Temp. (°C) + 17.78	1.8	Temperature (°F)
	Temp. (°F) − 32	.555	Temperature (°C)
	Temp. (°C) + 273	1	Absolute temperature (°C)
	Temp. (°F) + 460	1	Absolute temperature (°F)
Concentration units	$EC \times 10^3$ (= electrical conductivity in millimhos per centimeter)	10	Milliequivalents per liter, approximate only (in range 0.1 to 5.0 millimhos per centimeter)
	$EC \times 10^3$	640	Parts per million, appoximate only (in range 0.1 to 5.0 millimhos per centimeter)
	$EC \times 10^3$	0.36	Osmotic pressure (in range 3 to 30 millimhos per centimeter)
	$EC \times 10^3$	0.87	Tons per acre-foot
	Grams per liter	0.8327	Pounds per 100 gallons
	Parts per million	1.0	Milligrams per liter
	Parts per million	0.00136	Tons salt per acre-foot water
	Parts per million	2.72	Pounds salt per acre-foot water
	Tons per acre	20.8	Grams per square foot
	Tons per acre	1000	Grams per 48 square feet
	Pounds per acre	.002296	Pounds per 100 square feet
	Pounds per square foot	43,560	Pounds per acre

(Source: Homer D. Chapman and Parker F. Pratt. *Methods of Analysis for Soils, Plants, and Waters.* University of California, Division of Agricultural Sciences, 1961.)

References and Additional Reading

Bailey, L. H. 1914. *The Standard Cyclopedia of Horticulture*. Macmillan, Inc., New York.

Bickford, E. D., and S. Dunn. 1972. *Lighting for Plant Growth*. Kent State University Press, Kent, Ohio.

Brent, A. C. 1976. *Modern Potting Composts*. George Allen & Unwin Ltd., London.

Cathey, H. M., and L. E. Campbell. 1978. *Interior Gardening*. U.S. Department of Agriculture, Home and Garden Bulletin 220.

Eckbo, G. 1950. *Landscape for Living*. McGraw-Hill, Inc., New York.

Flacker, W. J., and H. T. Hartmann. 1981. *Plant Science: Growth, Development and Utilization of Cultivated Plants*. Prentice-Hall, Inc., Englewood Cliffs, N.J.

Furuta, T. 1974. *Environmental Plant Production and Marketing*. Cox Publishing Co., Arcadia, Calif.

_____. 1978. *Properly Placed Plants Can Reduce Energy Use*. Cox Publishing Co., Arcadia, Calif.

Graf, A. B. 1970. *Exotica*, Roehrs Company, East Rutherford, N.J.

Hortus Third. 1978. Macmillan, Inc., New York.

Joiner, N. N., ed. 1981. *Foliage Plant Production*. Prentice-Hall, Inc., Englewood Cliffs, N.J.

Laurie, Alex, D. C. Kiplinger, and K. S. Nelson. 1979. *Commercial Flower Forcing*, 8th ed. McGraw-Hill, Inc., New York.

Neal, Marie C. 1965. *The Gardens of Hawaii*. Bishop Museum Press, Honolulu.

Robinette, G. O. 1972. *Plants/People/and Environmental Quality*. U.S. Department of the Interior, Washington, D.C.

Simonds, John O. 1961. *Landscape Architecture, the Shaping of Man's Natural Environment*. McGraw-Hill, Inc., New York.

Sommer, Robert. 1969. *Personal Space. The Behavioral Basis of Design*. Park and Recreation Administrators Institute, Asilomar, Calif.

Index
to Plants

General Index

A

Abnormal plant growth, 121–122
Acanthus family, 130–131
Acetic acid, 131
Adapted plants, 129–130
Air conditioning, 65, 78, 81
Air pollutants, 80
Air pollution, 80–81
Air-filled porosity, 85, 87
Algae, 40, 92, 123
Aphids, 117, 119, 123
Apical meristems, 41
Architectural uses of plants, 14, 17
Aspects of design, 24
Asymmetrical designs, 24
Attitude toward plants, 15–16, 98–99
Automatic irrigation system, 114

B

Bacteria, 40
Balance, 32

Bark, 85, 86
Base plane, 34
Begon, Michael, 137
Bonsai, 15, 145
Botrytis, 120
Bromel, Olans, 137
Budding, 43
Bulk density, soil, 85, 87

C

Calcined clay, 86
Calcium oxalate crystals, 131, 132
Cambrium, 41
Carbohydrates, 52, 60
Cation-exchange capacity, 87
Cell division, 41
Characteristics of plants, 31–38
Charcoal filter, 81
Chelated fertilizer, 101, 102
Chemicals to control plant growth, 43
Chlorophyll, 52